Early Christianity and Historical Methods

Early Christianity and Historical Methods

Repudiating the Contemporary Approach

Joel Steele

RESOURCE *Publications* • Eugene, Oregon

EARLY CHRISTIANITY AND HISTORICAL METHODS
Repudiating the Contemporary Approach

Resource Publications
An Imprint of Wipf and Stock Publishers
199 W. 8th Ave., Suite 3
Eugene, OR 97401

www.wipfandstock.com

PAPERBACK ISBN: 978-1-6667-0093-0
HARDCOVER ISBN: 978-1-6667-0094-7
EBOOK ISBN: 978-1-6667-0095-4

04/20/21

One of the first duties of man is not to be duped, to be aware of his world: and to derive the significance of human experience from the events that never occurred is surely an enterprise of doubtful value. To establish the facts is always in order, and is indeed the first order of the historian; but to suppose that the facts, once established in all their fullness, 'will speak for themselves' is an illusion.

—CARL BECKER

Contents

Preface | ix
Abbreviations | xi
Introduction | xiii

1. ΠΡΟΣ ΦΙΛΙΠΠΗΣΙΟΣ (To the Philippians) | 1
   Historical Background | 2
   Literary Context | 3
   Exegetical Analysis | 4
   Application(s) | 13
   Textual Critical Interpretation of Philippians 2:1–11 | 16

2. New Testament Canon | 17
   Apostolicity and Orthodoxy | 18
   Consensus | 22

3. Apostolic Succession | 26
   Irenaeus | 27
   Historiography | 28
   Irenaeus's Motives | 31

4. Inerrancy of Scripture | 35
   God's Word | 36
   Biblical Accuracy | 37
   Science and Scripture | 39
   Case Study | 42

5. History and Theology | 46
Historians | 47
The Reliability of the Gospels | 48
The Gospel According to Matthew | 50
Interpretations of the Resurrection | 56
Historical Methods | 60

Conclusion | 62
Bibliography | 67

Preface

THE FOCUS OF THIS analysis centers on the work of early Christians, prominent theologians, and church historians who have developed and established orthodoxy in Christian theology. Apologetic approaches are analyzed and problems are shown to emerge when there is a lack of distinction made between historical and theological methods. Apologists who approach the study of history the same way they approach theology do both disciplines a disservice. The second part of the narrative argues that Christ is the essence of faith, i.e., this entity is a deity that exists only through faith. Christ's miracles, his resurrection, and atonement are not consistent with expected realities in history. Moreover, these elements of the deity were never intended to be proofs in a historical sense. Reason, therefore, in this context is not humanity's salvation. Nothing can be learned about Christ from history; he is a paradox, as Kierkegaard argued—Christ cannot be known (from a historical perspective). However, spiritual truths have been developed and can be learned through the Christian faith. Unlike Christ, the historical Jesus can be studied and limited knowledge about him has been discovered through historical inquiry—excluding all ties to the supernatural. This book will be especially alluring for those interested in understanding some of the most influential developments of early Christianity that morphed into components of the Christian doctrine. It is not a devotional book. It does, however, address textual analysis of ancient writings, historical approaches to studying theology, and methods used for historical inquiry. Emphasis is placed on historical methods and why it's important to distinguish theology from history. Perhaps the most controversial piece is in the last chapter; evidence is introduced by primary sources that question the current dating of one of the Synoptic Gospels.

Abbreviations

acc.	accusative
adj.	adjective
adv.	adverbial
aor.	aorist
art.	(definite) article
attrib.	attributive
BDAG	Bauer, W., F. W. Danker, W. F. Arndt, and F. W. Gingrich. *Greek-English Lexicon of the New Testament and Other Early Christian Literature*. 3rd ed. Chicago: University of Chicago Press, 1999.
BLB	Blue Letter Bible. https://www.blueletterbible.org
comp.	comparative
cond.	conditional
conj.	conjunctive
def.	definite
fem.	feminine
gen.	genitive
impf.	imperfect
impv.	imperative (mood)
inf.	infinitive

masc.	masculine
neut.	neuter
pl.	plural
sg.	singular
trans.	Transitive
UBS	Aland, Barbara, et al., eds. *The Greek New Testament: A Reader's Edition*. Stuttgart: Deutsche Bibelgesellschaft, 2017.

Introduction

THIS BOOK IS DESIGNED to introduce the foundation of early Christian theology and advocate for a distinction between history and theology. It is not an in-depth study of systematic theology, nor does it conduct a comprehensive account of the institutional developments, but it seeks to disclose the origins of Christian theology—the source of authority for the early church, i.e., Scripture. The decision was made and considered appropriate to begin with an ancient letter from a source responsible for the advancement of Christianity—originally known as Saul of Tarsus, although perhaps better known as St. Paul, chief of the apostles. A critical examination of specific passages in the letter to the Philippians reveal the primary christological issue that became controversial for the early church fathers. An exegetical analysis provides the reader with an unintentional emergence of systematic theology by the author (Paul) pertaining to the nature of Christ and his position in the Godhead. The first chapter regarding this issue is primarily for those with advanced knowledge of the Greek language. However, an English translation is provided for all Greek passages. Nevertheless, for those concerned who are unfamiliar with Greek, forgoing the first chapter will in no way impair the reader's ability to comprehend and follow the narrative.

The exegetical analysis of Paul's letter to the Philippians concludes with a theological application, priming chapters 2–4, which are devoted to ancient Christian developments that profoundly affected Christian theology, i.e., the formation of the canon, apostolic succession, and inerrancy of Scripture. The canon's development was a critical source integrated with the history of the ancient church. Likewise, the development of apostolic succession was important; it assisted the church with their struggle against heresies. A short historiography of the inerrancy of Scripture is introduced because equally important as the establishment of the canon and apostolic succession was the reliability of Scripture. Understanding specific developments of church history is an important aspect to the study of historical theology. Historical theology evaluates historical events and situations where various theological ideas were developed and formulated. However, it is important to distinguish between the disciplines—history, theology, and the study of historical theology. The last chapter addresses apologetic issues pertaining to supernatural claims made in the past that are connected to theology. A distinction is made between studying the paradoxes of a central phenomenon at the heart of Christianity (Χριστός) and the historical inquiry of Jesus as a man.

1

ΠΡΟΣ ΦΙΛΠΠΗΣΙΟΣ (To the Philippians)

In Paul's letter to the Philippians, after the salutation, which includes Timothy, Paul expressed his gratitude for the Philippians' dedication to the Christian faith, and prays for their continued growth and grace. This epistle reveals an affectionate attitude toward his recipients in Philippi. Philippi was a city in Macedonia and a Roman colony (Acts 16:12). The Philippians were the first congregation to be established as a result of Paul's preaching in Europe. Paul was writing his letters to the Philippians while imprisoned in Rome or in Ephesus. He reassures the Philippians that his imprisonment has not hindered his ability to spread the gospel. In fact, Paul contends that "it has become known throughout the palace, and to everyone else, that my imprisonment is for Christ" (Phil 1:13). Moreover, this letter contains theological elements central to the Christian faith. Paul depicts Christ as being "in the form of man" while also sharing "equality with God." Paul himself appears to be conflicted regarding his hopes pertaining to the outcome of his trial. He knows that his death will result in being with Christ, but there are also benefits to remain alive, for the sake of the Philippians (Phil 1:23–24). Nevertheless, Paul encourages the Philippians to maintain spiritual unity through humility and love, according to the example set by Christ. Paul introduces what may have been part of a hymn regarding the incarnation of Christ in Philippians 2:5–11.[1] This exegetical inquiry will attempt to understand the meaning of the passages in Philippians 2:1–11 through textual analysis. It will also disclose the theological applications relevant to Christology. This part of the analysis will complement developments and advances made by the church fathers in the proceeding chapter(s). It is not necessarily a prerequisite for understanding the narrative.

Historical Background

Before plunging into the exegesis process, being familiar with the historical and cultural issues of the time, as it relates to Paul and his recipients, is a necessity. This will ensure the exegete has placed the material into the proper context, thereby enabling a more accurate meaning of what the author intended. Paul was writing nearly two thousand years prior to the twenty-first century. The Koine Greek with which Paul penned his letters provides cultural challenges to present-day English readers.[2]

In Paul's letter to the Christian community in Philippi there exists a mutual affection toward his recipients unlike other letters to the churches where problems would arise among the congregates. It is impossible to know Paul's exact location when he constructed the letter. Paul was, however, in prison and awaiting trial when he wrote the letter. Traditionally, scholars have placed him in Rome at the time of writing this letter. However, more recently some scholars have placed Paul's composition in Caesarea before his arrival in Rome or Ephesus at an earlier stage in his career. It is approximation to location that has many scholars leaning toward Paul being in Ephesus when he wrote the letter. Rome was about 800 miles to Philippi, and Caesarea was even further away from

1. Metzger, *New Testament*, 272–73.

2. Schreiner, *Interpreting the Pauline Epistles*, 50–51.

Philippi at nearly 1,200 miles, but Ephesus was only about 300 miles away from Philippi—a week by sea.[3]

Two of the primary cultural and historical influences to consider for this analysis is that Paul was fluent in the Greek language and familiar with Hellenistic thought. This is relevant because it discloses Paul's unique ability to express doctrines and the teachings of Jesus, based on the Old Testament, that would have been foreign to Gentiles and introduce them in a way which the pagans could understand. Moreover, Paul was a Roman citizen. His citizenship allowed him to travel broadly with minimal risk and access to the upper classes of society. Paul traveled through Asia Minor and Greece preaching the gospel and planting churches. The geographical area concerning this study is in northern Macedonia in the city/Roman colony of Philippi.[4]

Literary Context

This passage in Philippians reflects an important theological element critical to the Christian faith. Paul disclosed how Christ chose a reduction in status, "taking the form of a slave, being born in human likeness . . . he humbled himself and became obedient to the point of death, even death on a cross" (Phil 2:7–8). Christ is shown to be equal to God, but chose to reduce himself by taking on human form and giving his life on the cross for the sake of glorifying the father/himself bringing redemption to humanity. This is evident in verse 11: "and that every tongue should confess that Jesus Christ is Lord, to the glory of God the Father." Moreover, there is evidence that there are some who are troubling the Philippian church. Paul encourages them to stand firm in one spirit, with one mind. Yet, not through conceit or their own interests. Paul gives Christ's example of humbling himself in service in the Christological hymn of 2:5–11.[5]

3. Osiek, "Letter of Paul to the Philippians," 2099.
4. Shelly, *Church History*, 21–23.
5. Brown, *Introduction to the New Testament*, 177.

There are references to Christians singing hymns. However, the New Testament does not contain a book of hymns. There is no definitive way to detect hymns; nothing in the context explicitly states that a hymn is being introduced in this passage. There exists, however, among scholars a developed criterion for detecting a hymn. This includes: rhythmic style, parallel patterns, lines or strophes of equal length; the redactional addition of explanatory clauses or phrases to traditional hymns relates them more directly to the author's theme. The phrase "even death on the cross" in Philippians 2:8 is an example. Further, most scholars believe Paul wrote this passage, commonly known as "the Christ Hymn," but he was not the originator of the lines. Debates on Christology pertaining to 2:6–7 have ensued on whether the hymn postulates an incarnation of a divine figure or Christ is a human who was in the image of God, but humbly chose a reduction in status and was ultimately exalted by giving him the divine name in 2:9–11.

So, how does this passage fit into the greater context of the letter? The hymn is christological, but advises its recipients to, for their own salvation, follow the now exalted Christ.[6] For example, the Philippians are experiencing internal disharmony. Paul's primary concern is to bring them together. Therefore, he used a hymnic passage that praised Christ's self-emptying, even to death on a cross (humility). Christ's humility resulted in God's exaltation of him—giving him "the name that is above every name." This example Paul provided was to encourage the Philippians to empty themselves of their own selfish opinions and turn from partisanship to unity.[7]

Exegetical Analysis

Εἴ τις οὖν παράκλησις ἐν Χριστῷ.

The passage contains four εἴ clauses connected to τις depicting the work of God in the recipients' lives. Εἴ is a marker of a condition,

6. Raymond E., *Introduction to the New Testament*, 178–79.

7. Osiek, "Letter of Paul to the Philippians," 2009–2100.

existing in fact or hypothetical; it can be used to denote assumptions relating to what has already been established.[8] For example, "*since* there is . . ." The indefinite pronoun τις can be translated: "anyone," "someone," "a certain," or "a(n)."[9] In this case it is used to denote measurement, i.e., "be or amount to something" as an adj., "some, any, a certain."[10] "Therefore, if there is *any* . . ." However, when the decision is made to translate εἴ as "since" the Greek word τις can be omitted in English. This provides an English translation equivalent to the Greek meaning "Therefore, since there is . . ." There are few options for translating the meaning of the Greek word παράκλησις. 1. Act of emboldening another in belief or course of action, encouragement, exhortation. 2. Strong request, appeal, request. 3. Lifting of another's spirits, comfort, consolation. BDAG has this verse in Philippians listed under option 3—comfort or consolation.[11] UBS translates it as "encouragement" in the footnotes.[12] Εν Χριστῷ "in Christ."

Εἴ τι παραμύθιον ἀγάπης.

Here the Greek word παραμύθιον is translated as "comfort/incentive" in the footnotes of UBS.[13] ἀγάπης (gen. sg. fem.) "from love." Εἴ τις κοινωνία Πνεύματος, εἴ τινὰ σπλάγχνα καὶ οἰκτιρμοί. The Greek word κοινωνία is translated as "fellowship" in USB. BDAG defines it as "close association involving mutual interests and sharing, association, communion, fellowship, close relationship." Moreover, Phil 2:1 is listed as "fellowship with the Spirit" in BDAG under the first definition.[14] Πνεύματος has several meanings. However, in this context, it's obvious that the word does not represent breath, wind, or a part of human personality. In context of the theme Paul

8. BDAG, 277a.
9. Wallace, *Greek Grammar*, 347.
10. BDAG, 1008b.
11. BDAG, 766.
12. UBS, 526.
13. UBS, 526 note 19.
14. BDAG, 552.

is reciting, the meaning clearly has a divine element, and all who belong to God possess or receive this spirit—a distinction between Christians and unbelievers.[15] Paul expounded on the difference between spirit and soul in 1 Cor 2:13–15 pertaining to spiritual and unspiritual. The spiritual person knows God and has received the Spirit of God.[16] σπλάγχνα is defined as affection and οἰκτιρμοί is defined as "compassion" in the footnotes of UBS.[17] Thus, the meaningful English translation for this passage: "Therefore, since there is encouragement in Christ, since there is consolation from love, since there is sharing in the Spirit, since there is affection and compassion . . ."

πληρώσατέ μου τὴν χαράν, ἵνα τὸ αὐτὸ φρονῆτε.

The Greek word πληρώσατέ comes from πληρόω. *Vine's Complete Expository Dictionary* defines it as "to fill," in the passive "to be made full."[18] BDAG definition 3: "to bring to completion that which has already begun, complete, finish. Phil 2:2 is included in this definition."[19] The Greek pronoun μου is translated "my" in English. The article τὴν is omitted when translated from Greek to English. χαράν is acc. sg. fem. "joy." Considering the previous and following passages, it's clear that Paul is expressing that his joy will be complete—if the Philippians stay on a path of unity and humility in Christ. Thus, "make my joy complete." The epexegetical ἵνα clause is used after a noun or adjective to explain or clarify.[20] αὐτὸ is acc. sg. neut. BDAG definition 3: "pertaining to something that is identical with, or closely related to, something—the same."[21] φρονῆτε from φρονέω translated in the footnotes by UBS as "feel."[22]

15. BDAG, 834(5a).
16. Elwell, *Evangelical Dictionary of Theology*, 1134.
17. UBS, 526 notes 21, 22.
18. Vine, Unger, and White, *Vine's Complete Expository Dictionary*, 117a4.
19. BDAG, 828 def. 3.
20. Wallace, *Greek Grammar*, 476.
21. BDAG, 153 def. 3.
22. UBS, 526, note 23.

BDAG definition 1: "To have an opinion with regard to something, think, form/hold an opinion, judge."[23] Thus, "be of the same mind . . ." The rest of this passage functions in the same manner and the same criteria applies with minor exceptions. τὴν αὐτὴν ἀγάπην ἔχοντες, σύμψυχοι, τὸ ἓν φρονοῦντες. The Greek ἔχοντες from ἔχω, meaning to possess or contain, *have*, own.[24] The Greek τὴν αὐτὴν ἀγάπην, as explained previously, translates to English as "the same love." Thus, "having the same love." σύμψυχοι from σύμψυχος "united in spirit" and φρονοῦντες from φρονέω pres. nom. "think."[25] However, as previously indicated, BDAG provided an extended, detailed definition to include "to have the same opinion." Thus, the meaningful translation in English for the latter part of the passage: "make my joy complete: be of the same mind, having the same love, being in full accord and of one mind."

μηδὲν κατ᾽ ἐριθείαν μηδέ κατά κενοδοξίαν.

The Greek word μηδὲν "do nothing." κατ᾽ from BDAG definition 5: "marker of similarity or homogeneity, according to, in accordance with, in conformity with according to." This passage is specifically listed under definition 5b.[26] ἐριθείαν is defined as "selfish ambition" in the footnotes of UBS.[27] κενοδοξίαν acc. sg. fem. defined as "conceit" in the footnotes of UBS.[28] The Blue Letter Bible (BLB), relying on Strong's lexicon, defines it as: "empty glorying, i.e., self-conceit:—vain-glory."[29] Thus, "Do nothing from selfish ambition or empty conceit . . ." ἀλλὰ τῇ ταπεινοφροσύνῃ ἀλλήλους ἡγούμενοι ὑπερέχοντας ἑαυτῶν. The Greek words ἀλλὰ τῇ can be translated "but the." However, the article is omitted when translating to

23. BDAG, 1065 def. 1.
24. BDAG, 420 def. 1.
25. UBS, 526, notes 24, 25.
26. BDAG, 512–13 def. 5b.
27. UBS, 526, note 26.
28. UBS, 526, note 27.
29. G2754—*kenodoxia*, Strong's Greek Lexicon (NIV), Blue Letter Bible.

English. ταπεινοφροσύνῃ is dat. sg. fem., defined by BLB as "with humility of mind, having a humble opinion of oneself; a deep sense of one's (moral) littleness; modesty, humility, lowliness of mind." [30] The concept of humility became fundamental for Christian ethics.[31] Augustine stated: "If you ask me what is the first precept of the Christian religion I will answer first, second and third, Humility."[32] UBS defines it as "humility" in the footnotes.[33] ἀλλήλους is acc. pl. masc. and occurs sixty-seven times.[34] BDAG defines it as "each other, one another, mutually."[35] ἡγούμενοι is defined as "to engage in an intellectual process, think, consider, regard."[36] ὑπερέχοντας from υπερέχω "be of more value than."[37] ἑαυτῶν plural pronoun "yourselves."[38] Thus, a meaningful English translation of this passage: "Do nothing from selfish ambition or conceit, but in humility consider others as better than yourselves."

μὴ τὰ ἑαυτῶν ἕκαστος σκοπουντες
ἀλλὰ καὶ τὰ ἑτέρων ἕκαστοι.

Σκοπουντες from σκοπέω "be concerned about."[39] Keeping with the theme of humility and unselfish ambitions or desires, in this passage Paul continued to urge his recipients: "Let each of you look not to your own interest, but to the interest of others."

30. G5012—*tapeinophrosynē*, Strong's Greek Lexicon (NIV), Blue Letter Bible.

31. Hellerman, *Philippians*, 100.

32. Elwell, *Evangelical Dictionary of Theology*, 581.

33. UBS, 526 note 28.

34. G240—*allēlōn*, Strong's Greek Lexicon (NIV), Blue Letter Bible.

35. BDAG, 46.

36. BDAG, 434 def. 2.

37. UBS, 526 note 30.

38. G1438—*heautou*, Strong's Greek Lexicon (NIV), Blue Letter Bible.

39. UBS, 526 note 31.

τοῦτο φρονεῖτε ἐν ὑμῖν ὃ καὶ ἐν Χριστῷ Ἰησοῦ·

As previously disclosed, φρονεῖτε from φρονέω meaning "to have an opinion with regard to something" or "to give careful consideration to something, set one's mind on, be intent on" or "to develop an attitude based on careful thought, be minded/disposed."[40] The last definition is preferred—BDAG has this passage listed under this definition. Thus, "having this attitude or mindset," i.e., the same mind in you as was in Christ. The meaningful English translation: "Let the same mind be in you which was also in Christ Jesus . . ."

From this point in the letter Paul begins to articulate a concept that became foundational to Christian theology. Paul writes on the established position and status of Christ in the Godhead, which will be important for the development of systematic theology, although it's doubtful this was his intention. Paul's agenda, however, according to some scholars, was sociological not ontological.[41] Paul was focused on what Christ chose to do with his status as a divine entity.

ὃς ἐν μορφῇ Θεοῦ ὑπάρχων οὐχ ἁρπαγμὸν
ἡγήσατο τὸ εἶναι ἴσα Θεῷ.

The Greek word μορφῇ is translated as "form, outward appearance, shape."[42] The UBS translates it as "very nature."[43] This word pertains to the status Christ chose to take. The relationship that Jesus Christ had with God and the law he issued for humanity generally has two states—humiliation and exaltation. The incarnation was a form of humiliation; Christ chose to lower his status and take human form.[44] He did not regard equality with God as something to hold on to, i.e., exploit, or as "a thing to be grasped for selfish

40. BDAG, 1065–66 defs. 1, 2, 3.

41. Hellerman, *Philippians*, 105.

42. BDAG, 659.

43 UBS, 526 note 33.

44. Elwell, *Evangelical Dictionary of Theology*, 1147.

purposes." The NIV translates μορφῇ as "being in the nature of God."[45] ὑπάρχων is concessive and must be translated as "although he existed." As such, ἁρπαγμὸν is translated as "a thing to be grasped."[46] Still, translating it as "exploited" does not detract from the meaning. It's apparent that Christ's position could have been used for his own advantage. ἡγήσατο is translated as "regard" in UBS.[47] Thus, the meaningful English translation: "who, although he existed in the form of God, did not regard equality with God as something to be exploited . . ."

ἀλλ' ἑαυτὸν ἐκένωσεν μορφὴν δούλου λαβών, ἐν ὁμοιώματι ἀνθρώπων γενόμενος· καὶ σχήματι εὑρεθεὶς ὡς ἄνθρωπος.

The Greek word ἐκένωσεν from κενόω is defined as "to make empty, to empty."[48] This passage should be put into context with the previous passage, where Paul is explaining that Christ, though equal to God, was not selfish by seeking to retain his position, but was willing to reduce his status. Thus, Christ chose to "empty" or reduce himself of his prestigious position and take on human form. μορφὴν defined as "form, outward appearance, shape."[49] δούλου translates to "a slave."[50] λαβών art. act. sub. sg. trans. "taking on."[51] Christ did not actually take the form of a slave. In the ancient world, slavery was the most shameful status—an extremely low position in society. The recipients of Paul's letters would have understood this; it was an attempt to show the largest possible gap from someone who was already on the same level as God. Christ "emptied his glory by veiling it in humanity."[52] The rest of the passage harkens back to

45. "Who being in very nature," Phil 2 (NIV), Blue Letter Bible.
46. Wallace, *Greek Grammar*, 634.
47. UBS, 562 note 35.
48. BDAG, 539 def. 1b.
49. BDAG, 659.
50. G1401—*doulos*, Strong's Greek Lexicon (NIV), Blue Letter Bible.
51. G2983—*lambanō*, Strong's Greek Lexicon (NIV), Blue Letter Bible.
52. Wallace, *Greek Grammar*, 630.

the true meaning of Christ's reduction in status, not as being literally a slave, but referencing his humanity: ἐν ὁμοιώματι ἀνθρώπων γενόμενος· καὶ σχήματι εὑρεθεὶς ὡς ἄνθρωπος. "being born in human likeness. And being found in human form . . ." This positions the next passage, which disclosed Christ's supreme humility. The meaningful translation is: ". . . but chose a reduction in status, taking the form of a slave, being born in human likeness."

ἐταπείνωσεν ἑαυτόν γενόμενος ὑπήκοος
μέχρι θανάτου, θανάτου δὲ σταυροῦ.

". . . he humbled himself and became obedient to the point of death, even death on a cross." When Christ humbled himself, he became subject to obey the law from the Old Testament which God had commanded of his people. Jesus Christ followed the law with perfect obedience as a man; this he accomplished without the miraculous assistance from his divine powers, but from the strength of his human nature. This was a necessity; he had to be fully human to become the sacrifice for humanity's sin. Still, he himself, in his human form, did not sin. Moreover, he remained fully God when he took on human nature and was incapable of being conquered by death. Christ's humiliation reached its zenith at his trial, crucifixion, and death. Jesus' physical body died, fulfilling the role of propitiatory sacrifice; it was a requirement in order to bear humanity's penalty.[53] Hence Paul's attestation in this passage: "he humbled himself and became obedient to the point of death, even death on a cross."

53. Elwell, *Evangelical Dictionary of Theology*, 1147–48.

διὸ καὶ ὁ Θεὸς αὐτὸν ὑπερύψωσεν καὶ
ἐχαρίσατο αὐτῷ τὸ ὄνομα τὸ ὑπὲρ πᾶν ὄνομα.

The Greek word διὸ is translated: "therefore, for this reason."[54] ὑπερύψωσεν from ὑπερυψόω "exalt to the highest position."[55] The Greek word ἐχαρίσατο is from χαρίζομαι, defined by Strong's as: "to grant as a favor, i.e., gratuitously, in kindness, pardon or rescue:—deliver, (frankly) forgive, (freely) give, grant." Translated as: "Therefore God also highly exalted him and gave him the name that is above every name . . ."[56]

ἵνα ἐν τῷ ὀνόματι Ἰησοῦ πᾶν γόνυ κάμψῃ
ἐπουρανίων καὶ ἐπιγείων καὶ καταχθονίων.

The Greek word γόνυ is translated "knee" and κάμψῃ from κάμπτω 3rd sg. aor. act. sub. "will bow."[57] ἐπουρανίων from ἐπουράνιος defined as "heavenly, what pertains to, or is in heaven."[58] ἐπιγείων καὶ καταχθονίων translated: "on earth and under the earth."[59] Meaningful translation: "so that at the name of Jesus every knee should bend, in heaven and on earth and under the earth . . ." This passage parallels with Isaiah 45:23, where God states: "To me every knee shall bow, every tongue shall swear." Once again Paul has disclosed the equality Christ shares with God.

54. BDAG, 250.

55. UBS, 527 note 4.

56. G5483—*charizomai*, Strong's Greek Lexicon (NIV), Blue Letter Bible.

57. UBS, 527 notes 6, 7.

58. Vine, Unger, and White, *Vine's Complete Expository Dictionary*, 298, def. 2.

59. UBS, 527 notes 9, 10.

καὶ πᾶσα γλῶσσα ἐξομολογήσηται ὅτι Κύριος
Ἰησοῦς Χριστός, εἰς δόξαν Θεοῦ πατρός.

The Greek word ἐξομολογήσηται from ἐξομολογέω translated "confess."[60] Meaningful translation: ". . . and that every tongue should confess that Jesus Christ is Lord, to the glory of God the Father." This parallels to the second half of verse 23 in Isaiah 45: "To me every knee shall bow, every tongue shall swear."

Application(s)

Paul's letter to the Philippians was written in the first century. In the passages analyzed here, Paul's primary focus was an appeal to unity and humility through the example of Christ. This application may be appropriate in modern times, i.e., Christians should model their lives according to Christ's example—putting away selfish ambitions and looking to the interests of others. However, perhaps the most significant theological application is introduced in Paul's description of Christ's nature—choosing a reduction in status and taking on human form, being obedient to the law, offering himself as the sacrifice for humanity's sinful debt by dying a physical death on the cross. This was the ultimate humiliation of Christ (mentioned in what is now known to modern readers as verse 8), demonstrating one of the two states of Jesus Christ. He was fully God and became fully human. He experienced ultimate humiliation on the cross to the point of death—in his human form. Jesus Christ's resurrection began the process of exaltation. Christ was exalted upon resurrection along with his human nature. His human body was in a much more glorious state—no longer subject to death. Christ, as the second person in the Trinity, was also exalted. Upon his resurrection, God the Father was satisfied with Christ's work of redemption and he returned to his original divine status—equality with God.[61] Hence, Paul's attestation: "Therefore God also highly exalted him and gave him the name that is above every name . . ." (Phil 2:9).

60. UBS, 527 note 11.

61. Elwell, *Evangelical Dictionary of Theology*, 1148–49.

Although Paul's intention was not to provide a systematic theology pertaining to the Godhead, the concepts that he had articulated in this passage of the epistle to the Philippians would be (or at least should have been) foundational for the future of the church's doctrine and defense against heresies. For example, while attempting to defend monotheism, various church fathers seemed to unintendedly compromise the full deity of Christ or his priesthood. In the third century, however, Tertullian and Origen affirmed that the Son always existed with the Father but implied a subordinate deity of the Son.[62] In *Against Praxeas*, Tertullian used terminology such as "three persons" and "one substance," which became acceptable language for expressing the doctrine of the Trinity.[63] Origen used the term *logos*—the Son of God, who became human in Jesus. Roger Olson explains, "Logos, according to Origen, is somehow less than the Father, although he never explained exactly what that means."[64] However, the Nicene Creed implies the Father and Son are equal: ". . . begotten, not made, being of one substance with the Father . . ."[65] Still, Origen was of two minds. On one side Origen subordinated the Son to the Father. On the other side, he favored equality of the Logos with the Father, and this was the side that Christians in training at Alexandria promoted regarding Origen's Christology.[66]

Greek philosophy was at the heart of the dispute between Arius and Alexander over the nature of Logos.[67] One reason is that people related to terms used in Greek culture because it had explanatory power, especially for those who thought as Platonists—a real universe above individual things, much like Plato's theory regarding forms. This was why Basil and the Gregories though it important to explain what they meant by the term *hypostasis*.

62. Arand, Nestingen, and Kolb, "History of the Ancient Creedal Texts," 23–24.

63. Ferguson, *Church History*, 1:127.

64. Olson, *Story of Christian Theology*, 142–43.

65. Nicene Creed, "Christian Classics Library," line 7.

66. Olson, *Story of Christian Theology*, 143.

67. Olson, *Story of Christian Theology*, 143.

Hypostasis is occasionally used for "substance" in Greek culture.[68] The Council of Constantinople, called by Emperor Theodosius in 381, declared that true Christian orthodoxy must include that Jesus Christ was both truly God and truly human. For the most part the debate over the Trinity was settled.[69] The bishops' adjuration to the authority of the Roman Empire, which had its own motivations to settle the matter, supports the narrative that the church fathers used their influential positions—a tactic Irenaeus implemented regarding heresy he attached to the Gnostics—to develop an orthodox Christian religion evident in the Nicaean Creed.

Moreover, many scholars have associated Paul's description of Christ in this passage as paralleling with Adam and the "fall of man" in Genesis. Essentially, Jesus Christ is the second Adam—the antithesis to the first Adam, whose disobedience and "fall" represented humanity as a whole.[70] In Genesis 3, Adam attempted to secure for himself divine attributes, thereby forfeiting the glory he had been given along with any further glory God may have intended for him.[71] In contrast, as mentioned, Christ "emptied himself" or humbled himself by first taking on human form, demonstrated perfect obedience in his earthly life, and experienced the ultimate humiliation by dying on a cross, thereby, being "highly exalted by God and given the name above every name." In his letter to the Philippians, Paul used Christ's life as a model. He encouraged his recipients to imitate Christ's humility. Further, as mentioned, the concepts Paul used to convey his message to the Philippians would have unforeseen benefits pertaining to unharmonious christological views within the church.

68. Olson, *Story of Christian Theology*, 185.

69. Olson, *Story of Christian Theology*, 197.

70. Bryce, "Christ as Second Adam," 358–59.

71. Bryce, "Christ as Second Adam," 366.

Textual Critical Interpretation of Philippians 2:1–11

1Therefore, since there is encouragement in Christ, since there is
consolation from love, since there is sharing in the Spirit, since
there is affection and compassion, 2make my joy complete: be of
the same mind, having the same love, being in full accord and of
one mind. 3Do nothing from selfish ambition or conceit, but in
humility consider others as better than yourselves. 4Let each of
you look not to your own interest, but to the interest of others.
5Let the same mind be in you which was also in Christ Jesus,
6who, although he existed in the form of God, did not regard
equality with God as something to be exploited, 7but chose a reduction in status, taking the form of a slave, being born in human
likeness. And being found in human form, 8he humbled himself
and became obedient to the point of death, even death on a cross.
9Therefore God also highly exalted him and gave him the name
that is above every name, 10so that at the name of Jesus every knee
should bend, in heaven and on earth and under the earth, 11and
that every tongue should confess that Jesus Christ is Lord, to the
glory of God the Father.

2

New Testament Canon

THE NEED FOR A canon was realized when various religious sects (Gnostics, Marcionites, and Montanists) distorted and fabricated religious ideas pertaining to Jesus and the Hebrew Bible. Some heresies that influenced the development of a canon were: Marcion, and the Marcionite canon; Gnostics, and their document the Nag Hammadi; and Montanus, with the two prophetesses. An origin of authority could be used as a guide and applied externally to heretics and internally within Christianity. Eventually, the worthiness of certain books emerged from a process. The developmental process partially rested on historical and theological tradition from early accounts—the apostles. The development of the New Testament canon was not merely the nature of dogmatic assertion; it was a gradual process that eventually disclosed the worthiness of certain books based on orthodoxy, apostolicity, and consensus among the churches.[1]

The developmental process involved choosing and excluding certain books. For example, the Nag Hammadi documents, which includes authors claiming to be apostles, were not incuded in the canon because they were deemed unworthy for various reasons: not adhering to orthodoxy, not having characteristics of apostolicity, or they created other problems—late dates compared to

1. Metzger, *Canon of the New Testament*, 251–54.

the Gospels in the Christian canon, that is, the list of books the church fathers had in their possession but had not yet approved. The Gnostics used their document to support their semblance of a Christian religion. They also claimed to have secret teachings passed down from the apostles. The church fathers developed their canon to rebuke the heretic's version. They refused to allow Scripture to be interpreted in a random fashion; it was crucial for Scripture to be interpreted within the context of orthodoxy and historical continuity of the Christian church,[2] thus revealing an important interrelation between the approval of books and the developmental process.

Among the list of books the church fathers possessed, Didymus provides basically the same list of books as Athanasius. This suggested a criterion for consensus among the churches. Marcion, who was not considered fully Gnostic, developed a canon but it was selective and based on Gnostic influences.[3] The church fathers responded to heresy with their list of unapproved books, which would eventually become the New Testament canon. They gradually came to an agreement of specific books found to be worthy of the canon based on orthodoxy, apostolicity, and consensus.

Apostolicity and Orthodoxy

Eventually, the churches most likely would have officially confirmed a list of canonical Christian writings on their own.[4] Bruce Metzger, former professor at Princeton Theological Seminary, has written extensively on the influences and development of the New Testament canon. Metzger's work is still considered among the most influential in New Testament scholarship. Metzger used the texts from the Nag Hammadi, discovered in 1945 in Egypt, along with the knowledge of Gnosticism derived from patristic writers to extract the Gnostic religious belief system. It turns out that the

2. McGrath, *Historical Theology*, 37–38.

3. Metzger, *Canon of the New Testament*, 98.

4. Shelley, *Church History*, 69.

documents from the Nag Hammadi verified what the church fathers had expressed in their writings regarding the Gnostic's view. These discoveries present a detailed account of the problems the orthodox churches faced.[5]

The Gnostics rejected the Old Testament. Furthermore, they produced texts which they claimed were the apostle's report of a secret communication from the Lord exclusively for them along with alleged oral traditions passed down from the apostles to them. The church contested Gnostic views by pointing out that nothing in their claims can be found in the four Gospels. The Gnostics responded by directing them back to their source—secret traditions. The critical issue for the church was to determine what constituted the true gospel and legitimate apostolic writing. The church fathers initiated a process of extreme caution: not to accept anything unless it revealed genuine apostolic characteristics. Their decision restricted the Gnostics from exploiting claims of secret traditions. This decision also impacted the orthodox churches' oral tradition, which they sometimes preferred to books. However, to prevent the Gnostics from distorting Scripture the church insisted on the rule of faith for biblical interpretation.[6] The rule of faith, articulated by Irenaeus in *Against the Heresies*, essentially states: The church received the faith in one God, creator of heaven and earth, and in one Jesus Christ, the Son of God, who became flesh for our salvation through the physical death and resurrection. He ascended into heaven but will return to "recapitulate all things."[7]

The books found in the Nag Hammadi documents failed to specifically match the criteria set by the church fathers. The *Gospel of Thomas* is one example. Unlike the four Gospels, the *Gospel of Thomas* is not a narrative; it is a collection of the sayings of Jesus.[8] The strongest rebuke of Gnosticism was prevalent in Irenaeus's writings, who assisted in establishing the acceptance of orthodoxy regarding the four Gospels. Irenaeus was familiar with a wide range

5. Shelley, *Church History*, 76.
6. Shelley, *Church History*, 77–78.
7. Irenaeus, *Against the Heresies*, book 1, 49.
8. Meyer, *Nag Hammadi Scriptures*, 8.

of early Christian literature.[9] He appealed to symbolism found in creation, evident in his writings. Irenaeus insisted that there are only four Gospels just as there are four winds and four corners of the universe; no more, no fewer.[10] This was not the only reason to reject the *Gospel of Thomas*. For example, orthodoxy pertaining to apostolicity was solidified by Clement of Rome. Clement held that the apostles were made evangelists by Jesus Christ; Jesus was sent by God. In short, Christ is from God and the apostles are from Christ, and they are the foundation of the church.[11] There are a few scholars that contest the dating of the *Gospel of Thomas*, but most agree it was compiled about AD 140.[12] Thus, the primary reason to reject the *Gospel of Thomas* was that it failed to present authentic apostolic characteristics (the late date indicates it was a forgery). Metzger points out other issues with the false gospel. The examples used by Metzger revealed that although the *Gospel of Thomas* has passages that parallel the church's gospel, it contains a severe Gnostic twist to the canonical sayings of Jesus.[13] The following is an example provided by Metzger from a passage in the *Gospel of Thomas*: "Simon Peter said to them: Let Mary go away from us, because women are not worthy of life. Jesus said: Lo, I shall lead her in order to make her a male, so that she too may become a living spirit, resembling you males. For every woman who makes herself a male will enter into the kingdom of Heaven."[14] It was not easy for the church to defend against Gnosticism; to compound the problem, a wealthy Christian shipowner named Marcion had adapted some of the Gnostic's views.

Marcion was a respected member of one of the churches in Rome. He was known to have contributed large financial sums to the church. In AD 144 Marcion appeared before the clergy in Rome to present his teachings in hopes of winning over others to

9. Holmes, *Apostolic Fathers in English*, 93.

10. Meyer, *Nag Hammadi Scriptures*, 7.

11. Shelley, *Church History*, 69.

12. Metzger, *Canon of the New Testament*, 86 para. 1.

13. Metzger, *Canon of the New Testament*, 86 logion 37.

14. Metzger, *Canon of the New Testament*, 86 logion 114.

his point of view. Since none of Marcion's original work on his ideas has survived—what he called *Antitheses*—Metzger extracted contents found in Tertullian's writings against Marcion, which consists of five volumes. Marcion's primary ideas included the rejection of the entire Old Testament, two gods—one of the Old Testament and one of the New Testament—an edited version of Paul's epistles, and a selective Gospel of Luke. Paul was viewed as the only apostle to understand the significance of Jesus Christ's role in Maricon's Gnostic religious ideas. Thus, after editing any references to the Old Testament, he accepted Paul's writings as authoritative. Marcion rejected nearly all of the Gospels that the orthodox church had in their possession. Luke was the only Gospel that Marcion trusted because Luke was Paul's disciple; after some editing and omitting most of the first four chapters (for the sake of conforming to Marcion's ideas), the Gospel of Luke was included in Marcion's canon. The presbyters were stunned to hear Marcion's radical views. The assembly ended with the excommunication of Marcion and his money was returned.[15]

Gnosticism and the Marcion controversy demonstrate two things. First, it revealed that Marcion developed his canon out of a comprehensive list of books that the church already had in their possession. Second, the authority of apostolic writings was placed alongside the Gospel writings—this was seen through the contestation of Gnosticism by the church pointing out that Gnostic ideas are not found in any of the four Gospels. So, these heresies were not directly responsible for the New Testament canon, which have led some to mistakenly believe the development of the canon was merely a counterweight to the heresies of the day. The heresies were indirectly responsible because they accelerated the process of developing a formal canon, forcing the church to state more clearly what they already believed. It also disclosed a criterion for the canon's development: apostolicity and orthodoxy. Orthodoxy and apostolicity came into focus through the Churches' charge that Gnosticism ideas are absence in the Scriptures. Although Marcion developed Scripture-based ideas from apostolicity, borrowed from

15. Metzger, *Canon of the New Testament*, 90–93.

the Christian church's list of books, it was proven to be severely lacking and distorted because of selective passages and major edits.[16]

Consensus

Another influential movement that re-enforced the church fathers' position for the need of a canon of the New Testament was Montanism. Originating in Asia Minor, it spread through the whole church—East and West. Montanism claimed to be a religion of the Holy Spirit. Montanus was the religion's founder; after his conversion he fell into a trance and began to speak in tongues. He claimed to be inspired by a new outpouring of the Holy Spirit. He used the Gospel of John as a reference for his claim. Two married women, Prisca and Maximilla, left their husbands to join with Montanus and spread his message. The essence of the pew prophecy was that the heavenly Jerusalem would soon descend upon earth to the Phrygian town the three founders had settled in; there they uttered prophecies while conducting eccentric ceremonies. Didymus, the monk appointed by Athanasius as head of the Alexandrian catechetical school, reported some of the sayings of Montanus. These reports revealed that Montanus believed (or claimed) it was God who was speaking through him. Other reports disclosed that his two companions also believed they were an instrument that God used to speak through. The common theme was apocalyptic in nature—they were the final prophecy before the end.[17]

Initially, the church was confused as to how the movement should be handled. Montanus's preaching did not appear to be the work of the Spirit. A decision was made by bishops in Asia Minor that the new prophesy was the work of demons and should be cut off from the fellowship of the church. However, it was not a unanimous decision. The church experienced decades of uncertainty before a consensus emerged among them. Eventually, the bishop of Rome, the bishop Carthage, and the remaining African bishops

16. Metzger, *Canon of the New Testament*, 99.

17. Metzger, *Canon of the New Testament*, 101.

declared the Montanists a heretical sect. The Montanist movement created a mistrust of prophetical and apocalyptic literature among the church, leading to the discredit of several apocalypses that were in the possession of various churches. More importantly, the foundation of the Montanist movement, which insisted there was a continuous and ongoing inspiration of prophesy, initiated the first steps toward a closed canon by the church.[18]

Earlier Didymus was mentioned. He was used as a source that reported the sayings of Montanus to disclose the characteristics of the Montanist religion. Didymus was an important figure who can also be used to disclose a consensus among the churches pertaining to the list of books they possessed. Bart Ehrman is the James A. Gray Distinguished Professor of Religious Studies at the University of North Carolina, Chapel Hill. Ehrman argues that not enough attention has been given to the status of the canon in Alexandria during the fourth century. Ehrman uses Athanasius's thirty-ninth paschal letter to disclose the list of twenty-seven books Athanasius listed as canonical that would become universally accepted by the church. Ehrman then turns to the writings of Didymus, which reveal the methods he used to independently produce a list of books he considered canonical. Didymus viewed the canon as a collection of books that had been divinely inspired. Further, the divine authorship of these books is what produces unity among them. Therefore, the canon must not be a diverse collection of books that create tension, but a unified collection that reveals the teachings of God. This was part of the process Didymus used to discern which books should be included in the New Testament canon. Ehrman emphasizes that not every piece of literature that Didymus quoted from functioned as a verifiable interpretation of Scripture; only canonical books were used for this purpose. Didymus did use noncanonical literature. For example, historical accounts written by the Jewish historian Josephus were used by Didymus. Josephus recorded the destruction of the temple of Jerusalem and noticed it was the fulfillment of prophecy. Although true in the historical sense, there was nothing inspirational or authoritative in Josephus

18. Metzger, *Canon of the New Testament*, 106.

that Didymus considered canonical. Unlike other books, inspired books could be used to verify or support the passages of other inspired books—self-authenticating.[19] Didymus accepted most of the twenty-seven books Athanasius listed as canonical. This indicates a consensus derived independently from each source. However, there were a few additional books Didymus viewed as inspired and authoritative that were not part of the twenty-seven books Athanasius listed in his letter. Didymus's occasional quotations from the noncanonical books were only in passing. Ehrman argues that Didymus referenced other noncanonical books "because they independently concur with a theological or exegetical insight, in which case they are correct but not authoritative, or because they have something of philosophical or historical interest to say."[20] Note, the description of Didymus's reference to noncanonical books is not to prove he was in complete agreement on a New Testament canon. Didymus did fully accept most of Athanasius's list. Still, there were a few books not part of the twenty-seven which Didymus viewed as inspired and authoritative. The primary purpose for analyzing Didymus's distinction between canonical and noncanonical is to show a separation in the process of assertation. This is because the determination process Didymus used resulted in a close consensus with Athanasius. Later, Rufinus, who studied under Didymus, produced a list of canonical books that nearly matched Athanasius's list.[21] However, this consensus among the three did not confirm a canon for the church. The confirmation process of twenty-seven books that make up the current New Testament began at the Synod of Hippo Regius.

In 393, the Synod of Hippo was the first to formally accept a canon of the books of the New Testament. The Synod at Hippo decided on the canon based off the criterion presented above—orthodoxy, apostolicity, and consensus among the churches. The Synod of Hippo decreed: "Beyond the canonical scriptures

19. Ehrman, "New Testament Canon of Didymus the Blind," 1–6.

20. Ehrman, "New Testament Canon of Didymus the Blind," 6 para. 1.

21. Metzger, *Canon of the New Testament*, 233–34.

nothing is to be read in church claiming to be divine scripture."[22] They called on the bishop of Rome, Boniface, and other bishops to confirm the canon of books listed in the decree. Although the confirmation process began at the Synod of Hippo Regius in 393, it was not finalized until the Council of Cartage in 397.[23]

22. McDonnell, "Canon and Koinonia/Communion," 45 para. 3.
23. McDonnell, "Canon and Koinonia/Communion," 46, 48.

3

Apostolic Succession

THE EARLY CHURCH FATHERS viewed the doctrine of apostolic succession as a very important factor for the church. The apostolic traditions are the unwritten oral traditions of Christ's teachings passed down through the apostles. The word "apostle" comes from the Greek verb *apostellein*, meaning to send. Thus, an apostle is someone who is sent. In the New Testament the apostles were Jesus' disciples sent by him to spread the Christian message. For the early church fathers, apostolic succession was the way in which the true and only doctrine of Christianity could be preserved.[1] It would later serve as a political tool for establishing the papacy. When the "New Rome," was established in Constantinople, apostolic succession was promoted by the Western church as the foundation of authority for the church regardless of where the capital was located. St. Leo the Great was the primary figure who rejected the notion of changing the center of catholicity. He believed that since the gospel had been rejected by the Jews, it was preached to the pagans. Thereby St. Peter transplanted Jerusalem to Rome, "where he sealed his testimony with his blood, as did St. Paul."[2] Today, the Catholic Church still believes that tracing bishops back to Peter (Christ's disciple) is what provides them with

1. Benoit-Dominique and Miller, "Church Is Apostolic," 591–93.
2. Benoit-Dominique and Miller, "Church Is Apostolic," 603.

supreme authority over the whole church.[3] This chapter will argue why apostolic succession was important for the early church since the time of Irenaeus, and how it became misused by leaders of the Catholic Church, helping to usher in the Reformation.

Irenaeus

Known among modern scholars as the "first theologian," Irenaeus was a disciple of Polycarp, who was a disciple of the apostle John.[4] Thus, Irenaeus learned the Christian faith through the Johannine principles. This process also shaped his views on how the Christian message should be preserved; as a *traditio*, that is, "a thing 'handed down,' person to person, from the incarnate Christ to every generation of the faithful."[5] This tradition, apostolic succession, was important to establish during the apostolic age because it refuted Gnostic teachings, which made claims of secret traditions pertaining to Christ. To prevent the Gnostics from distorting Scripture, the church insisted on the rule of faith for biblical interpretation. Irenaeus's articulation of the faith, framed in this manner, became a popular method in the African battles against Gnostic movements.[6]

The strongest rebuke of Gnosticism is clearly seen in Irenaeus's writings, which also assisted in establishing the acceptance of orthodoxy regarding the four Gospels. Irenaeus was familiar with a wide range of early Christian literature.[7] He appealed to symbolism found in creation, evident in his writings. Irenaeus insisted that there are only four Gospels just as there are four winds and four corners of the universe; no more, no fewer.[8] This is an important concept pertaining to Scripture that would be used by

3. Benoit-Dominique, and Miller, "Church Is Apostolic," 594–96.
4. Steenberg, "Tracing the Irenaean Legacy," 199.
5. Steenberg, "Tracing the Irenaean Legacy," 201.
6. Steenberg, "Tracing the Irenaean Legacy," 204.
7. Holmes, *Apostolic Fathers*, 93.
8. Meyer, *Nag Hammadi Scriptures*, 7.

the Protestant Reformers to refute Roman Catholic primacy, as apostolic succession began to eclipse Scripture. However, orthodoxy regarding apostolicity, which is credited to Clement of Rome and agreed upon by the early church fathers, was that the apostles were made evangelists by Jesus Christ, who had been sent by God. Essentially, Christ is from God and the apostles are from Christ, and they are the foundation of the church.[9]

The origin of apostolic succession had been established (originating with Clement of Rome and Irenaeus), the influences that led to apostolic succession had also been established (Gnosticism), and criteria for the philosophy had been made known (Christ is from God and the apostles are from Christ, and they are the foundation of the church). The historiography of events related to apostolic succession within the church will not only disclose disagreements among the bishops of Western and Eastern churches, but will also disclose the divisions between Protestant and Catholic religious views, all of which continue today.

Historiography

During the second century it was inconceivable how the concept of apostolic succession would have been misused. However, with the Christianization of the Roman Empire came new problems within the church, many driven by political ambitions. After defeating Licinius, Constantine decided to move the empire's capital closer to Rome's most serious rival, Persia. He chose Byzantium because the location had natural defensive barriers. Once he had transformed Byzantium into the new capital, he changed it's name to Constantinople.[10] Political power shifted to the East, and the importance of Old Rome declined. Many churches began looking to the bishops of Constantinople for spiritual leadership. In a political move to boost the episcopal power in the East, a council was

9. Moriarty, "I Clement's View of Ministerial Appointments," 18–19.

10. Herrin, "City of Constantine," 5.

called by the new emperor to renew the Nicene Creed. It was primarily an Eastern affair; none of the Western bishops attended.[11]

The Eastern church was first met with serious opposition when Leo the Great established himself as head of all Christendom. He accomplished this through his sermons. Leo's sermons offered a coherent systematic Christology, which none of his predecessors had offered. Moreover, his sermons centered on St. Peter for conceptualizing the bishop's role in Christian theology. It's clear that Leo's convictions led him to believe he was the heir of the apostle Peter.[12] Thus, he laid the foundation for papal primacy by appealing to the destiny of Peter set by Jesus, who promised to build his church upon the Rock—Peter—for all ages. In Leo's view, the bishop of Rome was Peter's successor, who was charged with preserving Christian orthodoxy. This is an early case where apostolic succession was being used politically to gain dominance among the churches—not the way Irenaeus intended for it to be used. The Western church had a difficult time accepting a diminished role when Rome's new capital shifted the empire's power to the East. Apostolic succession was used as a tool for legitimizing the status of the Western church.

Roman-Byzantine Relations Deteriorate

The Greek and Latin churches continued their disagreements through letters of insults. They attacked each other's customs and closed churches that opposed theology that was not mainstream in the area; that is, Constantinople closed Latin churches. In one of the Greek letters, it appears the Greek church had received some of the emperor's support. These events resulted in a papal reply and action; most notably, in 1054, things came to a head. On July 16, 1054, Mass was in progress at the church in Constantinople. Unexpectedly, three papal legates entered the church and placed a document on the altar. As they were on their way out,

11. Barnes, "Emperors and Bishops," 182,

12. Salzman, "Leo's Liturgical Topography," 208–11.

they addressed the congregation in Latin, "*Videat Deus et judicet,*" meaning "Let God look and judge." The document was carried to the patriarchal palace, where it was discovered to be a bull of deposition and anathema against the patriarch himself.[13] Thus, the schism of 1054.

Over time, military losses and heresy weakened the Eastern empire, and in 1453 Constantinople fell to the Islamic Turks.[14] There were and still are many theological disagreements among the Eastern and Western churches. However, the misuse of apostolic succession is at the center of the Roman Catholic arrogance articulated by Leo the Great in his sermons during the fifth century, arguing only Peter's church (located in Rome) and the apostles' successors have the authority to lead the church and preserve orthodox Christianity.[15]

More Division in Christianity

"Unless I am convicted of error by the testimony of Scripture and plain reason, I cannot and will not recant anything, for to go against conscience is neither right nor safe. Here I stand, I cannot do otherwise."[16] These were the words of Martin Luther as he stood before the Diet of Worms, in 1521, to defend his stance against the Catholic Church for the practice of issuing indulgences. By Luther's time, Western Christianity had become a powerful political, intellectual, and financial institution. Along with the institution's rise in prestige regarding political and economic affairs, the Catholic Church experienced a sharp decline in morality. A failure in oversight by the bishops led monks and priests to engage in secular activity. The majority of people did not question the church's authority. However, a minority viewed many religious practices as misguided. They become known as reformers, those

13. Shelley, *Church History*, 150.
14. Haskell, "'Tristia' of a Greek Refugee," 110–11.
15. Mayne, "East and West in 1054," 133–36.
16. Wiesner-Hanks, *Early Modern Europe*, 164.

who encouraged people to spend their money on the needy and their time in prayer, as opposed to spending their money and time on pilgrimages, relics, or indulgences.

By reading the letters of Paul, Luther worked out a doctrine different from the Catholic one he had been taught. *Sola fide*, *sola gratia*, and *sola Scriptura* are Latin phrases translated: "faith alone," "grace alone," and "Scripture alone." This meant that justification came through faith, not good works; faith was a gift from God, not merit based; and, most applicable to apostolic succession, God's word is disclosed in Scripture alone, not tradition passed down by the church.[17] This newly developed doctrine, later known as the Protestant religion, was the sharpest theological divergence from both the Greek and Latin churches. The Reformation may have originated with Luther's Ninety-Five Theses against the church for selling indulgences, which was to pay for the construction of St. Peter's basilica in Rome. Nonetheless, Scripture alone became one of the most important concepts to emerge from the Reformation. Without the understanding of Scripture alone, the Catholic Church could simply appeal to Leo's understanding of apostolic succession by citing that authority must come from the source, a successor of Peter, who was chosen by Christ to build his church. Does Irenaeus's doctrine of apostolic succession align with the Roman Catholic's concept of it?

Irenaeus's Motives

The most significant threat to Christianity during Irenaeus's time was the Gnostics. Bruce Metzger, former professor at Princeton Theological Seminary, used the texts from the Nag Hammadi, discovered in 1945 in Egypt, along with the knowledge of Gnosticism derived from patristic writers to extract the Gnostic religious belief system. In his book *The Canon of the New Testament*, Metzger argued:

17. Wiesner-Hanks, *Early Modern Europe*, 164, 166–68

> . . . in defending itself against Gnosticism, a most important problem for the church was to determine what really constituted a true gospel and a genuine apostolic writing. In order to prevent the exploitation of secret traditions, which were practically uncontrollable, the Church had to be careful not to accept nothing that did not bear the stamp of apostolic guarantee . . . in order to prevent Gnostics from twisting the Scriptures, the Church would insist on the 'rule of faith' as the norm of Biblical interpretation.[18]

Irenaeus's purpose, evident in his writings, was to refute heresy and instruct those who wished to learn about Christianity. According to Everett Ferguson, professor emeritus of Bible and distinguished scholar-in-residence at Abilene Christian University, proof is found in Irenaeus's anti-heretical work, *Against Heresies*.[19] Irenaeus's warnings against false teachings in *Against Heresies* were clearly a response to the Gnostics, Docetism, and Marcionites. Specifically, he postulated three errors: putting a Father above the Creator, denying the incarnation, and rejecting prophecy—the Old Testament.[20] Moreover, as previously mentioned, his strongest rebuke of Gnosticism was the acceptance of orthodoxy regarding the four Gospels. Irenaeus was promoting apostolic succession as it related to Scripture; it was tradition, made problematic by the Gnostics, that had become less relied on by the church during this time. Metzger disclosed how the church dealt with the Gnostic teaching in the quote above. He also disclosed that an indirect consequence of the church's decision not to accept anything that did not bear apostolic succession "was a devaluation of oral tradition."[21] It does not appear that Irenaeus would hold the same concept of apostolic succession as the Catholic Church has since at least Leo the Great. Irenaeus's motives were not as politically fueled as the later Catholic Church's would become.

18. Metzger, *Canon of the New Testament*, 78.
19. Ferguson, "Irenaeus' Proof," 8.
20. Ferguson, "Irenaeus' Proof," 12.
21. Metzger, *Canon of the New Testament*, 78.

James White, theologian and contributor to the book *Sola Scriptura*, explains Irenaeus's statements regarding tradition. White focused on a particular passage in *Against Heresies*, which Roman Catholics use to support their claims regarding tradition, White extracts the following from Irenaeus's writings:

> On this account are we bound to avoid them, but to make choice of things belonging to the Church with the utmost diligence, and to lay hold of the traditions of the truth . . . For how should it be if the apostles themselves had not left us writings? Would it not be necessary [in that case] to follow the course of the tradition which they handed down to those to whom they did commit the Churches?[22]

White argues that the traditions Irenaeus speaks of are extra-biblical. Furthermore, Irenaeus defines what he means when he references tradition; he cites the rule of faith, which is:

> These have all declared to us that there is one God, Creator of heaven and earth, announced by the law and the prophets: and one Christ, the Son of God. If any one does not agree to these truths, he despises the companions of the Lord; nay more, he despises Christ Himself the Lord; yea, he despises the Father also, and stands self-condemned, resisting and opposing his own salvation, as is the case with all heretics.[23]

This is consistent with Metzger's evaluation of the early church fathers' defense against Gnostic teachings, which was developed to distinguish what really constituted a true gospel and a genuine apostolic writing. Thus, Roman Catholics, starting with Leo the Great (and his interpretation of why the bishop of Rome is considered Peter's successor, who bears the responsibility of preserving Christian orthodoxy and who is also the true authority on Christian doctrine), have misrepresented the patristic materials, specifically pertaining to apostolic succession. They engaged in

22. White, "Sola Scriptura and the Early Church," in Beeke et al., *Sola Scriptura*, 20.

23. White, "Sola Scriptura and the Early Church," in Beeke et al., *Sola Scriptura*, 21.

anachronistic interpretations, that is, the deconstruction of ancient literature for the purpose of inserting concepts and ideas into the original sources that were not intended by the ancient authors.[24]

Still, many Catholics today, of course, do not share the Protestant interpretation of apostolic succession. They still hold the "unwritten tradition," which they claim was handed down by Christ to the apostles or delivered by the Holy Spirit to the apostles, as equally important as Scripture.[25] Their response to the Reformation was developed formally at the Council of Trent, 1545–1563.[26] The following is an excerpt from the Council of Trent provided by Benoit-Dominique de al Soujeole supporting the Catholics' position on "unwritten tradition": "the unwritten traditions, which have been received by the apostles from the mouth of Christ Himself, or from the apostles themselves, at the direction of the Holy Spirit, have come down even to us, transmitted as it were from hand to hand."[27] Perhaps there is too much at risk, both politically and financially, for the Roman Catholic Church to relinquish this authority they have created exclusively for themselves.

24. White, "Sola Scriptura and the Early Church," in Beeke et al., *Sola Scriptura*, 32.

25. Benoit-Dominique and Miller, "Church Is Apostolic," 591 para. 2.

26. Wiesner-Hanks, *Early Modern Europe*, 187.

27. Benoit-Dominique and Miller, "Church Is Apostolic," 591 para. 2, "Council of Trent:"

4

Inerrancy of Scripture

THE STUDY ON INERRANCY is important to Christian theology because it relates to the trustworthiness of the Bible. Inerrancy supports the claim that Scripture is the inspired word of God. This is not viewed as important to the contemporary church as it has been to early Christianity. However, according to tradition, if the Bible is not shown to be fully truthful, the Christian view of inspiration would also be in endangered. Inerrancy was important to the early Christians because confronting these issues would also refute to their critics.[1] For example, it is important to disclose how the term *inerrancy* is not sufficient when describing the Bible's message. The term needs an explanation for the context in which it is used by most Christian scholars and theologians, rather than from the perspective of scientific exactness. From the perspective of scientific exactness, the Bible may appear to contain errors. However, these accusations would not extend into faith or the Christian message. The errors are inadvertent errors, not an indication of falsehood; in matters of faith and salvation the Scriptures have preserved religious truths. Thus, for Christians the Bible can be considered the inerrant word of God without committing to scientific exactness.

1. Erickson, *Christian Theology*, 194.

This chapter will include some of the most prominent theories on inerrancy from the past. Case studies will be analyzed to disclose the various opinions and progressions over time. Some of these studies include: Charles Augusts Briggs's heresy trial, Hermann Sasse's legacy in the Lutheran Church in Australia, and B. B. Warfield and his convictions on biblical inerrancy. Inspiration will be examined to determine how and to what extend the Scriptures are inspired. It is important to distinguish between inspired writings and noninspired writings of Scripture as it relates to inerrancy. Primary sources used will come from the Bible; they will be used to help support the secondary narrative—that the inspiration of writing Scripture, which was extended to the prophet or apostle by the Holy Spirit, was not a permanent phenomenon.[2]

God's Word

Albert Cook, former professor of theology in the Congregational College of Canada, argued that in the past God's communication with humans was descriptive rather that prescriptive. For example, if revelation is claimed to have originated from golden plates or stone tablets revealed through a prophet, this would only be a description of the circumstances, ultimately leaving the method unexplained. Divine revelation is no longer to be recognized in this manner if Christians are to receive the complete revelation of God. The reason for this is because too often a large part of the knowledge is human attainment, leaving only a small portion revealed by God.[3] Christians can recognize God's word or revelation independently of how it entered into human thought. God has no limits when it comes to communication. However, mortals are clearly limited in their communication skills. It is the Christian's duty to hear and obey God; to do so requires the Christian to recognize God's word when he hears it. There exist groups and organizations of many sizes that hold a variety of teachings, both

2. Erickson, *Christian Theology*, 180.

3. Cook, "Bible as God's Word," 127.

written and oral, pertaining to the revelation of God, each seemingly contrary to the other.[4] If it is God's desire to communicate his word to everyone, how is it possible that so many groups and organizations disagree with what God is communicating?

Cook insisted that one particular way God uses to communicate his word to one person may not apply to another. For example, the Hebrew and Greek version of the Bible has no value to the person who only understands English. This concept considers all characteristic of every individual. "For any given man no word of God is of any importance except that which relates to his needs and duties."[5] This does not encompass the universal truth of God's word found in Scripture. This applies to each individual according to their Christian duty and the method God uses to reveal his word to them. God will communicate with each individual in a way that is most comprehensible to that person.[6] Cook addressed why there may be different methods God uses for communicating or revealing his message to various people, but what about the revelation found in Scripture or the reliability of Scripture as a whole? There are some passages in the Bible that are seemingly contrary to historical or scientific accuracy.

Biblical Accuracy

The term *inerrancy* is not found in the Bible. Some people prefer not to use the term at all when addressing biblical claims. This is because the modern concept of inerrancy possesses a number of assumptions that would be foreign to the authors of the Bible. Mark Worthing holds a PhD in history and philosophy of science from the University of Regensburg and a ThD in ecumenical theology from the University of Munich. He investigated the inerrancy of Scripture debate within the Lutheran Church of Australia (LCA). Worthing used the ideas of Swiss Calvinist theologian

4. Cook, "Bible as God's Word," 128 para. 2.
5. Cook, "Bible as God's Word," 128 para. 3.
6. Cook, "Bible as God's Word," 130.

Francis Turretin and others to show various positions held regarding inerrancy. Turretin believed the Bible to be free from all errors because those that wrote it were inspired by the Holy Spirit. Lutheran Orthodox developed similar views. However, instead of using the term *inerrant*, they used the term *perfect* or *without error* when emphasizing the authority and truthfulness of Scripture. The difference was they sought to disclose that perfection or error-free matters applied only to faith and salvation, whereas Turretin had an all-encompassing view on the accuracy of Scripture. Turretin's view included religious matters along with historical and scientific references made by the biblical writers.[7]

Hermann Sasse was a Protestant theologian; he received his training in Berlin. He was instrumental to the ongoing LCA debate. He argued that within Lutheran tradition the inspiration and inerrancy of Scripture are implicit not explicit. Sasse believed that people should accept the means which God has chosen to speak to them. For Sasse, there was a clear distinction between divine inspiration and the human aspect in God's written word.[8] Still, he recognized the authority of Scripture, stating, "if the Holy Scripture does not exist as the source and norm of the Church doctrine, then there is no church doctrine and consequently there is no church."[9] Sasse's view is somewhat compatible with Cook's view regarding the method God chooses to communicate with various people. The debate that took place within the LCA was important because it continues to represent many positions today pertaining to inerrancy—some view all Scripture as inerrant; others believe the Bible's message regarding faith and Christian living to be error free but this perfection does not necessarily apply to scientific or historical matters.

7. Worthing, "Inerrancy of Scripture Debate," 57–58.

8. Noble, "Hermann Sasse's Theology of Scripture," 185, 188, 192.

9. Noble, "Hermann Sasse's Theology of Scripture,"192 para. 1.

Science and Scripture

Benjamin Breckinridge Warfield, former Professor of Didactic and Polemic Theology at Princeton Theological Seminary, was well known for believing that the Bible communicates revelation of God without error. Warfield was also known for his strongly held Calvinist views. Over the span of his academic career, he sought to make his Christian beliefs compatible with evolution. Warfield was a student of Charles Hodge at Princeton. He greatly admired Hodge, however, Hodge's views on evolution would test Warfield's admiration. Hodge published a monograph that attempted to define Darwinism. He identified it as the changing of species over time, modified through natural selection, and a transformation within the natural process without the "recourse to teleological forces."[10] All three identified characteristics of evolution defined by Hodge were compatible with the Christian theism, but the third one was not. Warfield appears to have fully embraced evolution during this period.

In the 1880s, American theologians were being drawn into debates by modern critics in Europe over biblical accuracy. Charles Briggs of Union Seminary in New York favored an updated view on tradition regarding the Bible. Warfield defended the fundamentalist view maintaining that the Bible was fully inspired, absolute, and without error. He argued that the Scriptures are a combination of divine and human activity that work harmoniously to produce a writing that is never lacking in the other—divine and human at once in every word.[11] Philosophically, this doctrine had immense potential for Warfield. A correlation could be made to disclose compatibility between the Bible and evolution; that is, the process of natural history could be the consequence of both occurring at the same time—natural forces and divine action.[12] Warfield's stance on evolution shifted over his career. He seemed to be a pure evolutionist early in his career, but over time he became suspicious

10. Livingstone and Noll, "Biblical Inerrantist as Evolutionist," 155.

11. Livingstone and Noll, "Biblical Inerrantist as Evolutionist," 157.

12. Livingstone and Noll, "Biblical Inerrantist as Evolutionist," 157 para. 4.

that evolutionary theory was no more than an explanatory process that fell short of proof. However, his primary concern was holding on to the idea that evolution and the inerrant word of God were not mutually exclusive. Warfield contended that mechanical explanations in nature were consistent with his Calvinist theology of divine creation.[13] However, is this an acceptable approach for Christian theists regarding the Bible, that is, to conform Scripture to harmonize with modern views?

J. Gresham Machen was a graduate of Princeton Seminary and influential proponent of the doctrine of biblical inerrancy. Furthermore, he was an advocate for B. B. Warfield's views on the inspiration and infallibility of Scripture. Machen argued that no matter how unbelievable and outdated, Scripture is authoritative and infallible. Therefore, it is the only guide for the church.[14] To make the text relevant to modern societies, many Protestant scholars added a developmental view to their studies. They used historicism—holding the view that a document is conditioned by its historical and cultural context. This was an attempt to spiritualize the meaning of biblical passages. The narrative would then be used to show apostolic teachings may not have provided an accurate description of religious truths. Instead, it disclosed religious truths from the perspective of the first century. Thus, with assistance from the social sciences biblical scholars were able to apply the Bible to contemporary issues, ushering in an improved biblical message for modern times. This new approach did not view the Bible as the standard to judge the present, but as a model for conforming the church to a contemporary setting. Machen argued that, by failing to accept Scripture on its own terms, this new approach consisted of predispositions held by modern men that would distort the ancient text.[15] For Machen much was at stake studying Scripture from this modern perspective. He believed studying the

13. Livingstone and Noll, "Biblical Inerrantist as Evolutionist," 163.

14. Hart, "Fundamentalism, Inerrancy," 13, 20.

15. Hart, "Fundamentalism, Inerrancy," 20–21.

Bible without acknowledging it as the word of God diminishes its authority, thereby making it nearly meaningless.[16]

Gregory Boyd is a theologian and the senior pastor of Woodland Hills Church in St. Paul, Minnesota. Boyd argues that many modern scholars have embracing a way of studying Scripture that excludes any involvement of faith, thereby approaching canonical writing the same way they would any ancient document. This approach can be traced back to Bible scholars during the nineteenth century who adopted a scientific model for the study of Scripture. In an effort to take an objective stance on the subject, academics viewed Scripture strictly through a historical lens. It was thought to be the only intellectually sound way to interpret Scripture because it was outside the authority of the church and assumed to be free of presuppositions. This undermined the church's traditional claim that the Bible was the inspired word of God. Further, there were many Christian theists who objected to this approach and preferred the traditional approach—understanding the Bible as God's inspired word. However, there were enough biblical scholars in academia that supported a strictly historical approach. Hence, much of the Christian scholarship on the subject was associated with modern fundamentalism.[17]

The inclusion of Boyd's analysis was not to advocate studying biblical history through a Christian presupposition, but to reveal the impact some of the nineteenth-century contemporary ideas had on the way the subject is now approached. Boyd's analysis appears accurate regarding traditional approaches to the study of Scripture; they are not always accepted as legitimate. Still, there is a sharp difference between what the academic scholars have classified as fundamentalism and understanding what inerrancy should imply regarding Scripture.

16. Hart, "Fundamentalism, Inerrancy," 26.

17. Boyd, "Interpreting Scripture as God's Word," 514–17.

Case Study

Charles Briggs was an ordained Presbyterian minister and Hebrew scholar. Briggs is best known for his challenge to the doctrine of the inerrancy of the original autographs. This doctrine stated that the original manuscripts that were the foundation for the Bible were completely free of error; it was the scribe or copyist who was responsible for any errors that may exist. Although Briggs published widely on his convictions, it wasn't until he was inducted into the Edward Robison Professorship of Biblical Theology that led to an investigation into his doctorial beliefs by the Presbytery of New York and Washington, DC.[18] Briggs believed the autograph idea lacked biblical and historical support. Moreover, it was a danger to Christianity because a proven error could result in evidence that Scripture lacks any inspiration from God and is merely the words of men. Essentially, Briggs advocated for admission of errors throughout Scripture. However, he insisted these errors were inadvertent and were of no consequence when it came to the biblical revelation of the Christian message.[19]

C. Frederick Wright was a professor at Oberlin in theological studies throughout the 1880s. He was a strong advocate for the inerrancy of Scripture and one of Briggs's strongest critics. When he challenged Briggs on the subject, Briggs used Matthew 27:9 as an example of an error—Matthew had credited a certain quotation to Jeremiah, when it was in fact Zechariah's words found in Scripture. Wright simply referred Briggs back to his inerrancy of autograph stance—stating it was more probable that the copyist made the mistake rather than the original author.[20] Ronald F. Satta conducted an analysis of the Briggs trial in the *Trinity Journal*. He summed up Briggs's position well: "The presence of errors in the Bible should neither surprise nor frighten students of Scripture, Briggs asserted. After all, it was written by fallible human beings, though to be sure under the general supervision of deity so its spiritual message

18. Satta, "Case of Professor Charles A. Briggs," 69.
19. Satta, "Case of Professor Charles A. Briggs," 70.
20. Satta, "Case of Professor Charles A. Briggs," 71.

retained full integrity."[21] Briggs maintained his position that errors existed not only in the copies but in the original manuscripts as well. He argued that inspiration extended only to the thoughts pertaining to the spiritual message of the Bible. Thus, inerrancy did not apply in matters of history, geography, and other scientific data.[22] The official position of the Presbyterian Church held that Scripture as written by the original sacred writers was absolutely free from any errors. In 1892, the Presbyterian Church tried and convicted Rev. Charles A. Briggs on heresy charges, that is, "teaching that errors may have existed in the original text of the Holy Scriptures, as it came from its authors . . ."[23] Today, fundamentalists are criticized and charged with heterodoxy for endorsing the doctrine of the inerrancy of the original autographs.[24]

Oral tradition has sometimes been more important than the written word for the Catholic Church, considering oral tradition is where the Catholic Church claims its authority, that is, through apostolic accession—passed down from the original apostles. Thus, their response to the Briggs controversy was not surprising. First, it should be noted that the Reformation did not occur on the basis of the infallibility of Scripture—Luther did not challenge the infallibility of Scripture; he challenged the infallibility of the church. R. C. Sproul explained the difference between the Protestant and Roman Catholic view in *Sole Scriptura*: The Catholic view—the Bible is an infallible collection of infallible books. The Protestant view—the Bible is a fallible collection of infallible books.[25] Thus, the predictable Catholic responds: "It is not enough that men be presented with the word of God, inerrant, truthful and inspired, they must moreover be possessed of an infallible means of reaching an inerrant, truthful and therefore inspired interpretation of it."[26] After a narrative on the importance of authority is established, it

21. Satta, "Case of Professor Charles A. Briggs," 72.

22. Satta, "Case of Professor Charles A. Briggs," 73.

23. Satta, "Case of Professor Charles A. Briggs," 75.

24. Satta, "Case of Professor Charles A. Briggs," 76.

25. Sproul, "Establishment of Scripture," in Beeke et al., *Sola Scriptura*, 41.

26. Nolin, "Briggs Controversy," 381 para. 2.

continues: ". . . authority, we say, set up by Christ in His church, not only to govern it, but also to hand down the holy traditions pure and intact, and to give to the divine word its true interpretation."[27] The lengthy response concludes with asking the question, "why should Dr. Briggs be singled out?" They argue that Briggs is simply acting in accordance with Reformed theology. Therefore, he has the right to attach whatever meaning to Scripture his private judgment suggests.[28] This somewhat satirical response was intended to disclose the importance of the (alleged) authority the Catholic Church was given by God.

Most scholars believe that early Christianity was spread through oral tradition with a fixed body of teaching. However, in 1 Corinthians 15:1–4, Paul provides a clear reference to the written passing of the Christian message. The reference to how he received the gospel is interesting; Paul uses the phrase "according to the Scriptures."

> Now, brothers, I want to remind you of the gospel I preached to you, which you have received and on which you have taken your stand. By this gospel you are saved, if you hold firmly to the word, I preached to you. Otherwise, you have believed in vain. For what I received I passed on to you as of first importance: that Christ died for our sins according to the Scripture, that he was buried, that he was raised on the third day according to the Scriptures. (1 Cor 15:1–4, Berean Study Bible)

The Christian message was written down a few decades after the death and resurrection of Jesus, allegedly. The message began to spread, creating a demand for copies. These copies accumulated to a massive number of resources for preserving the Scripture.[29] The next chapter will evaluate and perhaps challenge allegations pertaining to the dating of the Gospels.

Wright's use of the autograph idea to support the inerrancy doctrine may have had preservation issues. If the originals were

27. Nolin, "Briggs Controversy," 381 end of para. 2.

28. Nolin, "Briggs Controversy," 382.

29. McGrath, *Historical Theology*, 36.

truly error free, why couldn't God preserve them as they went through the copying process? Many argue that God did preserve his word. Of course, there are mistakes, but the Christian message is perfectly preserved. Briggs made some good points in his assessment of the inerrancy of Scripture. There was the human element to recording God's message. Furthermore, there is evidence that the authors were not continuously under the inspiration of the Spirit when writing. For example, Paul's words in 1 Corinthians demonstrate that inspiration was not a continuous process. "To the rest of you I say this (I, not the Lord): If any brother . . ." (1 Cor 7:12). In this passage, Paul differentiates between inspiration from the Holy Spirit and what Paul himself is saying. Sources like the one mentioned here support the narrative that the inspiration of writing Scripture, which was extended to the prophet or apostle by the Holy Spirit, was not a permanent phenomenon.[30] Thus, any exact references to science, chronology, or the like should not be held as inerrant; only inspiration provided by the Holy Spirit pertaining to godly living or the Christian message is what should be considered the inerrant word of God.[31] This argument is a logical defense. Still, many evangelicals hold to the theory that the autographs (the original manuscripts that no longer exist) are indeed without error.

30. Erickson, *Christian Theology*, 180.

31. Erickson, *Christian Theology*, 205, 208–9.

5

History and Theology

THIS CHAPTER COVERS THE resurrection of Jesus and what can be known about the resurrection from a historical perspective and the distinction between the disciplines of history and theology. To answer this question, an overview of what historians do will be discussed—common practices used to conduct a historical inquiry from the past. Once this is established, the reliability of the Gospels will be addressed. Finally, the analysis will cover the various interpretations of Jesus' resurrection, that is, claims made by scholars who refute the bodily resurrection of Jesus and adhere to hallucinations, visions, and metaphors as an alternative view of the narrative. The goal of this is to disclose what can be known about the resurrection and what most likely occurred in the past pertaining to this event. It's an important topic because the historicity of certain biblical claims before and after the resurrection support Christian theology. The material presented here strongly disagrees with most Christian apologetics' understanding of how historians should approach history. Much of their work, however, on refuting alternative claims to the bodily resurrection of Jesus is compatible with Christian theology.

Historians

Herodotus, an ancient Greek historian from the fifth century BC, is considered the father of history among historians. He sought to use verifiable sources to extract information from the past, developing the model that historians continue to follow today.[1] The issue with constructing a narrative of what occurred in the past is that it cannot be exactly replicated. Generally, this is because a considerable amount of information is missing—lost or destroyed. Historians construct fragments of the past and consider society and cultural influence when developing a narrative, filling in gaps based on historical evidence and producing an interpretation of the past. So, keep this in mind the next time you hear the phrase "What does the history tell us?" The history does not tell us anything. The historians tell us their interpretation of the past based on surviving fragments used to construct a narrative of what most likely happened. The following quote is from historian Carl Becker in the *American Historical Review*, from 1932.

> One of the first duties of man is not to be duped, to be aware of his world: and to derive the significance of human experience from the events that never occurred is surely an enterprise of doubtful value. To establish the facts is always in order, and is indeed the first order of the historian; but to suppose that the facts, once established in all their fullness, 'will speak for themselves' is an illusion.[2]

Historians will have a multitude of various interpretations of the past. Occasionally, these interpretations contain slight differences and at other times they are dramatically different. Hence, a vigorous debate among scholars is unavoidable, and some claim necessary, for the discipline.[3]

Historiography refers to the history of historical writing, in broad terms. Historiography in a narrower sense refers to the

1. Gilderhus, *History and Historians*, 5.
2. Becker, "Everyman His Own Historian," 26.
3. Brundage, *Going to the Sources*, 5.

specific area in history—the subject that will be investigated. Every topic has its own history.[4] However, the topic that will be addressed here, the resurrection of Jesus, has no definitive sources outside the New Testament. It should be noted that, ideally, historians prefer to use primary sources when constructing narratives and use secondary sources for support. Thus, it's important to be familiar with the literature available on the subject. As mentioned, there exists only one primary source for this investigation. However, there are some secondary sources and a vast amount of literature in circulation on the subject.

The Reliability of the Gospels

At first, when the Gospels are evaluated as a primary source they do not appear to pass as unbiased. However, there are other things to consider regarding this source and its biased views. Michael Licona is a scholar of the New Testament; he teaches apologetics at Houston Baptist University. In his book *The Resurrection of Jesus*, Dr. Licona contends that a hypothesis, in most cases, is probably adjusted to fit the facts, rather than looking for supporting evidence. Still, he asserts historians who are genuinely attempting to suppress their biased positions may possess a combination of the two.[5] Furthermore, recognizing that the past can be attainable to some extent by honestly questioning the information is crucial for anyone studying history. Licona had much to say on the historicity of the Gospels in a debate with Bart Ehrman. Licona argued that spiritual truths cannot be confirmed as historically reliable, nor can they be confirmed as unreliable because historians do not possess the tools needed to evaluate such claims. He gave the following example: "although historians are incapable of confirming that Jesus's death atones for sin, they can confirm that Jesus died by crucifixion."[6]

4. Brundage, *Going to the Sources*, 18.
5. Licona, *Resurrection of Jesus*, 107.
6. Licona, "Licona's Statement," Summary, para. 2.

Bart Ehrman is a distinguished professor. He teaches New Testament studies at the University of North Carolina, Chapel Hill. He argues that the earliest surviving sources containing information about Jesus comes from the apostle Paul. However, Paul did not personally know Jesus during the period of Jesus' life before the resurrection. So, the next earliest sources for information pertaining to Jesus are the Gospels of the New Testament. Ehrman contends these are the best available sources because they construct a narrative of Jesus' life. One problem, according to Ehrman, is that the sources are not written by eyewitnesses. The Gospels received their names—Matthew, Mark, Luke, and John—from Jesus' early disciples, who were all connected in some manner. Ehrman argues that the original followers of Jesus were uneducated Aramaic-speaking Jews, implying they were illiterate and could not have composed the Greek texts. Thus, these texts were not derived from someone sitting at the foot of Jesus taking notes.[7] Does this mean the Gospels are unreliable as a source?

Licona addressed the primary source Ehrman mentions in *The Resurrection of Jesus.* According to Licona, Paul's letters are verifiable reports disclosing eyewitness testimony of Jesus' resurrection. Furthermore, Paul knew some of the disciples who were eyewitnesses to the resurrected Jesus. Paul's conversion experience parallels the other eyewitnesses who claimed to have seen the risen Jesus. Licona argued that this substantiates the Gospels' claim regarding the resurrection and provides strong evidence for accepting these sources as reliable.[8] He also addressed Ehrman's argument that the Gospels did not come from the disciples—eyewitnesses—and that the text did not originate from someone sitting at the foot of Jesus taking notes, in a public debate with Ehrman. Licona compared ancient historical writings, specifically Plutarch's, and concludes the writers intended to write an accurate account of history. Licona demonstrated that Plutarch's accuracy on the writing of history significantly increases when the time is decreased from 800 years to about 150 years of his own time, and

7. Ehrman, *How Jesus Became God*, 89–92.

8. Licona, *Resurrection of Jesus*, 437, 439.

then pointed out the Gospels were written only thirty-five to sixty years after Jesus' death. Moreover, the eyewitnesses would have still been alive. Ehrman's claim that the texts did not originate from someone taking notes at the foot of Jesus was refuted by Licona. Licona argued Jesus most likely had sermons prepared that he taught over and over. Licona also pointed out that his disciples were with Jesus for three to five years. Hence, they would have heard the same teaching many times and would have been able to recite them verbatim. In fact, they were sent out by Jesus to teach these principles they had heard many times, and they taught them over and over.[9] This does not prove the Gospels were written by the eyewitnesses, but it does suggest they would be able to recall the information easily to communicate it orally and perhaps write it down later.

Another contention employed by contemporaries is that the Gospel writers used secretaries. However, comparing a Roman historian (Livy) who used a scribe to that of poor illiterate fishermen is not sufficient. Paul, who did use a scribe, was educated and Peter, who may have used a scribe, does not appear to be educated. Moreover, many scholars claim there is no evidence that either of these Christian followers were aware of the Gospels; the following section will challenge that claim by advocating for an earlier date of at least one of the Gospels.

The Gospel According to Matthew

As previously mentioned, many scholars argue that the authors of the Synoptic Gospels are unknown. It is believed that the names Matthew, Mark, and Luke were attributed to the books at some point for convenience. In 1 Corinthians, referring to Christ's atonement, Paul states, ". . . that he was buried, that he was raised on the third day in accordance with the Scriptures" (15:4). Paul's writings are dated to around AD 55. If the Gospels were dated, at the earliest, to AD 70, why would Paul be specific, mentioning

9. Ehrman and Licona, "Are the Gospels Historically Reliable?," YouTube, 16:40—17:30; 23:00—23:53.

"the third day"? The Old Testament does not directly foretell that Christ will be raised on "the third day." It seems Paul would have obtained this information from one of the Gospels not yet written, supposedly. Paul does not say "according to tradition," but "in accordance with the Scriptures." Thus, it is not likely that he was referencing oral tradition. Considering such, the Gospels appears to have been written much earlier than current scholarship claims. The focus here will be on the Gospel According to Matthew.

During the second century the Gospel of Matthew was quoted by the church fathers more than any other book in the church's possession. Before the canon, in Palestine, the Gospel According to Matthew was the only Gospel widely read.[10] Matthew contains more of Jesus' teachings than the other Gospels. However, scholars debate the book's date and actual author. Unlike the other two Synoptic Gospels, Mark and Luke, Matthew's Gospel has been traditionally contributed to one of the twelve disciples—Matthew. The hypothesis is that whoever wrote Matthew used Mark's Gospel as a source. This would place doubt on the authorship of Matthew's Gospel as actually having been written by the disciple Matthew. Why would an eyewitness to the events need to use Mark or any other source to write an account of events that took place? Inferences from the author's own writings are used to date when it was written. The date for the destruction of the temple in Jerusalem is known. Scholars interpret references to the temple by the author as somehow being aware that the temple has been destroyed. Thus, most date the Gospel of Matthew to be written after AD 70.[11]

There are some interesting things about the Gospel of Matthew. For example, Ignatius of Antioch wrote several letters to various churches, after his arrest and on his way to be martyred. There is a near-unanimous consensus among scholars that Ignatius was martyred AD 98–117.[12] In his letter to the Ephesians there is a reference of the virgin birth found in Matthew's Gospel:

10. Metzger, *Canon of the New Testament*, 262.

11. Cousland, *New Oxford Annotate Bible*, 1781.

12. Holmes, *Apostolic Fathers*, 170.

> Καί ἔλαθεν τόν ἄρχοντα τοῦ αἰῶνος τούτου ἡ παρθςενία Μαρίας καί ὅ τοκετός αὐτῆς, ὁμοίως καί ὁ Θάνατος τοῦ κυρίου· τρία μυστήρία κραυγῆς, ἅτινα ἐν ἡσυχία Θεοῦ ἐπράχθη.
>
> Now the virginity of Mary and her giving birth were hidden from the ruler of this age, as was also the death of the Lord; three mysteries to be loudly proclaimed, yet which were accomplished in the silence of God.[13]

This supports the claim that Matthew's Gospel must have been written during the first century because Ignatius cited it in his letter to the Ephesians before the end of the first century. Not many scholars disagree. However, there are other ancient sources that could be useful for dating Matthew's Gospel much closer to the beginning of the first century. Papias, bishop of Hierapolis in Asia Minor, provides some of the earliest information of the authorship of Matthew. It is not known exactly when Papias was born (Papias lived sometime during the last part of the first century and into the first part of the second century), but Irenaeus claims that Papias knew the apostle John. However, in *Church History*, Eusebius discloses that Papias himself, in the preface to his written work, indicated that he never had been a hearer nor had he met any of the apostles, but learned the faith through those who did know the apostles.[14] Only fragments of Papias's writings have survived. Eusebius provided some of Papias's writings in his history of the church. According to Eusebius, Papias describes Matthew's Gospel as:

> Ματθαίος μέν οὖν Ἑβραΐδι διαλέκτων τα λόγια συνετάξατο, ἡρμήνευσε δ' αὐτά ὡς ἠν δυνατός ἕκαστος.
>
> So, Matthew composed the oracles in the Hebrew language and each person interpreted them as best he could.[15]

13. Holmes, *Apostolic Fathers*, 196–99.
14. Holmes, *Apostolic Fathers*, 735.
15. Holmes, *Apostolic Fathers*, 741.

This contradicts what modern scholars believe. Most scholars believe that all the Gospels were originally written in Koine Greek. Nevertheless, in *Against Heresies* Irenaeus's remarks concur with Papias's claim regarding Mathew's Gospel being originally written in Hebrew.[16] The date currently given for the Gospel of Matthew was established by modern scholars under the assumption that the text was originally written in Greek. If the Gospel of Matthew was written in Hebrew, the dating of the text might be much earlier than scholars currently date it.

Many New Testament scholars believe that the disciples of Jesus consisted of poor illiterate peasants who would not be capable of constructing a literary narrative in Greek like the ones found in the Gospels. They contend that the disciples would have most likely spoken Aramaic based on the region they were from. What's interesting about this charge is that Hebrew and Aramaic are Semitic languages. It is not unlikely that Papias, Irenaeus, and Eusebius confused Aramaic with Hebrew. After all, the Hebrew Bible was translated into Greek—the Septuagint. This is because most of the early Christians during this era did not speak Hebrew. Moreover, the Hebrew language was not the primary language used by the Jews during the time of Jesus in Judea; they spoke Greek. Jesus, his followers, and the crowds he preached to most likely spoke Aramaic—a Semitic language closely resembling Hebrew.[17]

To address the issue pertaining to illiteracy, i.e., a large percentage of the population in antiquity was illiterate, specifically in the Palestine region, Matthew's occupation must be considered. The Gospel reveals that Matthew was a tax collector. To be efficient as a tax collector, the agent would have been required to evaluate the complexity of the region's economy as it related to Rome's demand for owed revenue. Trade that flowed locally and to other regions (exports) would have required an agent with the capacity to analyze and evaluate records of production for goods traded, e.g., metals, wheat, barley, wine, olive oil, etc. This would have required at the least basic skills in reading, writing, and

16. Irenaeus, *Against Heresies*, book 3, 30.

17. Cousland, *New Oxford Annotate Bible*, 1778.

math. Keith Hopkins's research on taxes and trade in the Roman Empire provides a good example of the complexity of the Roman economy.[18] An analysis from the second century indicates that the Roman Empire did not have adequate elite representatives for their providences. The empire relied on local officials to determine amounts owed in taxes and appoint local tax collectors.[19] This provides plausibility for the New Testament's claim regarding Matthew, i.e., he was a tax collector. Further, it can be deduced from Hopkins's research that a tax collector would require an education to perform duties associated with the complexities of the Roman economic system and collecting state revenue.

It is interesting that the church fathers made early use of Matthew's Gospel and that Matthew's Gospel was the Gospel primarily used by the church in Palestine. More intriguing are the claims that Matthew originally wrote his Gospel in Hebrew; at least that's what Papias and Ignatius seem to believe. Although, it makes more sense that Matthew was originally written in Aramaic—the Semitic language possibly mistaken as Hebrew. The early church fathers spoke Greek, as did the Jews in Judea at the time of Jesus. However, Jesus himself along with his followers spoke Aramaic. Matthew, a tax collector before becoming a disciple of Jesus, was most likely literate, as logic would have it—it would have been essential to carry out his duties as a tax collector for the Romans. Moreover, Paul's reference to Christ resurrection "on the third day in accordance with the Scriptures" suggests he was familiar with the Gospel writings. This provides additional support for the hypothesis that Matthew's Gospel was written much earlier than current scholarship has dated it. The reason(s): Paul's remarks in 1 Corinthians 15:3–4 not only indicate that he was familiar with the written Gospel, it discloses that since we know Paul was writing in AD 55 Matthew's Gospel would have had to have been earlier. James D. G. Dunn's research disclosed that the things which Paul received and passed on (referenced in this passage of Corinthians)

18. Hopkins, "Taxes and Trade," 101–4.

19. Hopkins, "Taxes and Trade" 121.

were actually formulated within months of Jesus' death.[20] Moreover, the language Paul uses in 1 Thessalonians 5:1–12 strongly resembles the language Jesus uses in Matthew 24:20–43, i.e., "thief in the night."

The issue of Matthew's Gospel being counted as Scripture during Paul's time is recognized. Nonetheless, the oral traditions were considered the gospel truth for early Christians during this time. So, without being officially canonized, it is possible that Paul would have recognized the writings, if indeed he was aware of them, as such. Further, a passage in 2 Peter discloses an explicit reference of one New Testament writer to another. Peter mentions Paul's writings, stating:

> ὡς καὶ ἐν πάσαις ταῖς ἐπιστολαῖς, λαλῶν ἐν αὐταῖς περὶ τούτων· ἐν οἷς ἔστι δυσνόητά τινα, ἃ οἱ ἀμαθεῖς καὶ ἀστήρικτοι στρεβλοῦσιν, ὡς καὶ τὰς λοιπὰς γραφάς, πρὸς τὴν ἰδίαν αὐτῶν ἀπώλειαν.
>
> . . . as in all the epistles, he [Paul] speaks of concerning this; in which are hard to understand, which the ignorant and unstable pervert, as also they do with the Scriptures, for their own destruction.[21]

Peter has categorized Paul's epistles with other writings, presumably those familiar to the readers, Scripture. If the author of this book (2 Peter) is accepted as Peter—one of Jesus' original disciples—this passage would suggest that Paul's writings were equally important as Scripture to those alive during their composition. It is also likely that the Gospel of Matthew would have been considered Scripture as well for those living during this same time. This would explain Paul's remarks in 1 Corinthians 15:4 and 1 Thessalonians 5:1–12.

20. Dunn, *Jesus Remembered*, 855.

21. My own translation of 2 Peter 3:16 from UBS.

Interpretations of the Resurrection

Michael Goulder was a scholar who taught biblical studies at the University of Birmingham. He appealed to psychological conditions for explaining the resurrection. Goulder argued that Peter was so overwhelmed with guilt and grief that his encounters with Jesus after his death were hallucinations rather than physical encounters. Peter shared his experiences with other followers, who began to have similar experiences in groups. Goulder tried to explain why Paul converted to Christianity by claiming that Paul felt restricted and in bondage to the Jewish law—Judaism—and this caused him to hallucinate. Thus, Goulder concluded that the resurrection never occurred; all the accounts by the sources are explanted away as hallucinations. Over time, gaps in the story were filled with exaggerations such as the empty tomb and bodily appearances.[22]

Since most historians will not appeal to the supernatural as the explanation, Goulder searched for a natural explanation for the resurrection of Jesus. However, the explanation that Goulder provided is very radical and does not represent sound historical methods for evaluating history. Essentially, the evidence for his claim relies on a psychoanalysis of historical figures living two thousand years ago. He was making guesses of what he thought may have happened to support his narrative rather than relying on the evidence to explain what most likely happened. Or, Goulder developed a narrative and looked for evidence to support it, and the best that could be produced was a psychoanalysis.[23] Opposing Goulder's psychosis claim, Licona argued that the American Psychological Association has shown it is unlikely for people to experience group hallucinations because generally they occur in a single mode.[24] Goulder's claim that Paul's conversion experience was due to his having second thoughts about Judaism that led to hallucinations also negates the evidence. In fact, Paul was a staunch opponent of Christianity; his mission had been to crush

22. Licona, *Resurrection of Jesus*, 479–82.

23. Licona, *Resurrection of Jesus*, 487.

24. Licona, *Resurrection of Jesus*, 483.

the church. Licona contended that Paul's experience and conversion were a result of encountering the physically risen Jesus.[25] Moreover, Paul's companions shared elements of his experience—they saw the light and heard the voice—not something normally associated with hallucinations or apparitions. Licona provided an excellent assessment of the immense issues with Goulder's psychosis claim. However, when Licona argued that Paul's experience stemmed from encountering the "risen Jesus," the narrative transitioned into a theological claim, not a historical one. It is only historically accurate in the sense that Paul and his companions testified to this event—they apparently believed they experienced a supernatural event. Nevertheless, historians do not have a way to evaluate such claims and will not engage with supernatural claims, whether they are religious or otherwise. This does not mean historians are excluded from practicing religion, but it is impossible to use historical methods to substantiate religious beliefs pertaining to the supernatural.

John Dominic Crossan is a scholar who opposes the literal interpretation of the resurrection. Crossman argues that a literal interpretation of Jesus' resurrection would be a "stumbling block" to non-Christians, keeping them from the Christian faith. Furthermore, Crossman believes it is nearly impossible for modern historians to know if a report was intended to be literal or metaphorical.[26] Licona disclosed there are many problems with the metaphoric interpretation of Jesus' resurrection; here are a few: The tomb of Jesus was under Roman guard. Jesus' followers were originally confused and upset to find the tomb empty. Hence, the body was missing. They would not have been upset or confused over a metaphor regarding an empty tomb. They knew he was dead and they knew where his body was being kept.[27] Licona argued that in 1 Corinthians 15:35–54 Paul refers to two types of bodies, earthly and heavenly. However, Paul made it clear regarding the resurrection that he uses the terms *perishable* and *imperishable* to

25. Licona, *Resurrection of Jesus*, 477.

26. Licona, *Resurrection of Jesus*, 519, 543.

27. Licona, *Resurrection of Jesus*, 544.

describe the physical resurrection of the body. It's clear the physical body is what will be resurrected and made imperishable.[28] He would not have distinguished between the two types of bodies had the language intended to be metaphorical. For example, metaphorically speaking the spiritual body will be resurrected and so will the physical body; it makes no sense to metaphorically speak of metaphors. Anyone attempting to claim that Jesus' resurrection was a metaphor has an *enormous onus probandi* to contend with considering the evidence. For example: Paul's companions who saw the light and heard the voice, the reactions of Jesus' followers when they learned of the empty tomb, and the encounter shortly after the resurrection where Jesus offered to let his followers touch him and eat with him. They metaphorically touched him and ate with him, and Paul's companions metaphorically experienced some of what Paul did during his encounter with Jesus at his conversion? That would be an extreme position given the evidence available that's nearly overwhelming in favor of the belief in a physical resurrection of Jesus by his followers. From a historical perspective, this narrative is evaluated only by what is recorded in the ancient text, i.e., what his followers claimed occurred; it does not consider the legitimacy of these supernatural claims. However, in accordance with orthodox Christian theology, the resurrection was physical.

Licona's narrative of the resurrection contains a supernatural component that he suggests historians refrain from making a judgement on one way or the other. He illustrated that if we are "bracketing" a worldview regarding his resurrection hypothesis, and assuming supernaturalism is false, then the resurrecting hypothesis would be implausible.[29] However, according to Licona, if the supernatural is accepted as a possible cause (God or a supernatural being desiring to raise Jesus from the dead), his resurrection hypothesis is very plausible. Licona argued that the historian should neither discount the supernatural nor consider it as a presupposition, but weigh the evidence and choose the one that has

28. Licona, *Resurrection of Jesus*, 545.

29. Licona, *Resurrection of Jesus*, 601.

the best explanation. Essentially, he was advocating that miracles not be ruled out by historians. Licona created some criteria for identifying a miracle: The phenomenon must be extremely unlikely considering the circumstances, and the phenomenon must occur in an environment "charged with religious significance." He insisted historians are warranted for accepting his hypothesis that Jesus physically rose from the dead.[30] Note, apologists often dismiss all the natural theories as a cause for the resurrection and accept the supernatural. Licona suggests as much in *The Resurrection of Jesus* when contemplating conflicting views on the subject and how each side would reject the evidence if it failed to support already held beliefs.[31] Unlike apologists, historians do not have the luxury of such practices. Again, it is never permissible for historians to accept the supernatural as the cause for an event because it is impossible to evaluate such claims. Likewise, the historian must refrain from conjecture—attempting to prove a supernatural event did not occur. It is impossible to prove that the resurrection did not occur.

Bart Ehrman agrees with many of the historical claims pertaining to Jesus. For example, Jesus died by crucifixion, it was their belief in the resurrection that led his followers to the belief that Jesus is the Son of God, and Jesus' followers believed that Jesus was physically raised from the dead; Ehrman states: "that belief is a historical fact." Ehrman's point is that historians can discuss events regarding Jesus that are not miraculous and do not require faith to know. Ehrman also argues that historians do not engage in supernatural inquiries because it is impossible to know these things. He insists that "religious faith and historical knowledge are two different ways of knowing." Likewise, the historian cannot use their discipline to show that Jesus was not raised from the dead because when it comes to historical methods, they are of no value for establishing what happened regarding a supernatural claim.[32] Many Christian apologists who view themselves as historians do

30. Licona, *Resurrection of Jesus*, 602.

31. Licona, *Resurrection of Jesus*, 608–10.

32. Ehrman, *How Jesus Became God*, 132–33.

not accept this approach. They are not simply using history as a tool for gathering insights into theology; they are attempting to merge them—refusing to acknowledge there is a fundamental difference between the two disciplines.

Historical Methods

As previously stated, the historiography of a topic will have different narratives; some slight, some dramatic. A historiography of a topic in total agreement would be suspicious; there would exist only a one-sided view of the past event. A debate regarding differences on any given historiographical topic is what makes history dynamic rather than static. A good example is the primary difference in the historiography of what lead to World War II, i.e., "appeasement" or the Treaty of Versailles. Historians who adhere to appeasement argue that the European powers were so desperate to avoid another war, after the traumatic experiences from World War I, that they allowed Hitler to gain a great advantage through appeasement measures, hoping it would satisfy him. The British and French waited until it was too late to confront him. Thus, Germany had become a military threat because Hitler used this time to prepare and position Germany for war. Historians who argue the Treaty of Versailles was the cause of World War II argue that the treaty created territorial disputes in Germany, restricted access to raw material for German manufacturing, and inflicted dire economic conditions from the retribution payments that Germany was required to pay for the First War. Thus, this enabled radical leaders like Hitler to assume power with the promise of a better future for Germany. The historian who argues for the Treaty of Versailles as the cause of World War II acknowledges there is too much evidence to ignore the appeasement narrative, and vice versa. However, both narratives lead to the same conclusion—in 1939, Germany invaded Poland and World War II officially began.

The two explanations provided in this section for contemplating the history surrounding Jesus, that is, theology—accepting Jesus as the Christ—and history—understanding Jesus as a historical figure—are very different than historians who have different interpretations on historical events like the example provided regarding World War II. Historians do not adhere to the metaphysical or supernatural for an explanation. Scholars who practice merging the supernatural into the historical substratum may find support among the entertaining historical narratives found on commercial platforms equivalent to the History Channel's *Ancient Aliens*, *Haunted History*, etc., or perhaps with contemporary evangelical apologists who claim to represent the historian's view. Theological practices—doctrines developed by orthodox theologians—use nearly every supportive narrative of the historical record leading up to and following the resurrection to conclude, by faith, that Jesus the Christ rose from the dead. This is the discipline of theology! Moreover, most theologians consider historical practice to be a minor element within their discipline. For example, philosophy is relied on by theologians but only to the extent that it can assist in clarifying their theology. It is faith based on Scripture that is central to the discipline of Christian theology. History and philosophy are secondary, i.e., they are used as supportive roles within theology. It is the apologist who seems to have a difficult time separating the disciplines.

Conclusion

In Paul's letter to the Philippians, it's unlikely that his explanation of Christ's position in the Godhead was meant for the development of systematic theology. His argument, however, would have future implications for understanding Jesus' identity, i.e., being equal to God and being fully man and fully God. Considering Paul's explanation to the Philippians pertaining to the position and essence of the second person in the Trinity, it is surprising these applications were not sourced during the Arian controversy.

There are no formal, universally accepted criteria for admitting a book into the canon. A decisive criterion simply does not exist. The existing historiography pertaining to the development of a canon is fragmented and scattered.[1] However, the criterion extracted from the records shows an emerging pattern of consistency that was used by the church fathers. The lag in the developmental process was expedited by various heretical movements. The developmental process eventually disclosed the worthiness of certain books. The rejection of the Old Testament by the Gnostics proved to be a mistake. The church fathers understood that surrendering the Jewish foundation provided by the Old Testament was self-defeating. Thus, they accepted the Jewish Scriptures along with their Christian Scriptures. This was a lesson Marcion failed to recognize when he developed his heavily edited version of a canon. The Montanist movement had a different effect than that of Marcion. The former made known the need to emphasize the

1. McDonnell, "Canon and Koinonia/Communion," 51.

final authority of apostolic writing, whereas the latter motivated the church to state more clearly what they already believed through the development of the breadth of Christian literature they had in their possession. The first complete list of books that make up the current New Testament canon was found in an Easter letter written in 367 by Athanasius. The same list was published by the councils in North Africa at Hippo in 393 and finalized at Carthage in 397.[2]

Much could be said theologically regarding the role inspiration played in the New Testament's development. However, from a historical perspective the evidence shows that the Christian church created the canon, but it was not a matter of dogmatic assertion. The canon was a recognition of the writings that made their authority known based on the reoccurring themes seen throughout the period—orthodoxy, apostolicity, and consensus among the churches. If the books in question contained two of these characteristics—orthodoxy and apostolicity—and the churches agreed they did, they were recognized as canonical.

The ancient church was truly apostolic; it was a necessity. The original concept of apostolic succession defined by Irenaeus for the purpose of refuting heresies of his day was an effective tool. Moreover, it was based on Scripture and, as Metzger demonstrated, not founded solely on oral tradition. The misrepresented interpretation of Scripture developed by Leo the Great for political purposes continued to plague the church. His doctrine, articulated through the sermons he preached during the fifth century, regarding apostolic succession through Peter and Peter's church carried through the centuries and led to the Great Schism of 1054. However, the greatest division occurred in the sixteenth century when Martin Luther posted his Ninety-Five Theses. His doctrine, focusing on four areas—salvation by grace alone, in Christ alone, by faith alone, through Scripture alone—transformed all of Europe. For many, the Reformation revealed the misguided concept of apostolic succession that the Roman Catholic Church relied upon for their supreme authority. *Sola Scriptura* became one of the most important concepts to emerge from the Reformation.

2. Shelley, *Church History*, 74.

Without the understanding of Scripture alone, the Roman Catholic Church could simply appeal to Leo's understanding of apostolic succession by citing that authority must come from the source, a successor of Peter, who was chosen by Christ to be the foundation of his church. Clearly, apostolic succession is the process for knowing how salvation is secured. However, authority with respect to doctrine is not strictly reserved for successors of Peter and his church—the Roman Catholic Church. The teachings of the apostles are preserved in the New Testament. The New Testament itself demonstrates tradition and the process of securing salvation. It is this tradition that continues in the church in the context of apostolic succession.[3]

The view of inerrancy has dramatically changed over time. Consider the ministries of George Whitefield (December 27, 1714—September 30, 1770) and John Wesley (June 28, 1703—March 2, 1791). These two devoted their lives to preaching. However, neither devoted a sermon to defending the inerrancy of Scripture. They assumed that in matters of the Christian faith the inspiration and infallibility of Scripture were instinctive—the norm within society.[4] However, the subject has become highly debated today.

Fragments from the writings of the early church fathers seem to contest the current dating of the Gospel of Matthew—even the original language (Greek). Moreover, there has never been an adequate explanation for the language Paul used to specifically describe Christ's atonement and where he obtains this information: "according to Scripture" and "the third day." The language Paul used, e.g., "thief in the night" in his other epistles (1 Thess 5:1–9), further indicates he most likely was familiar with the Gospel of Matthew.

Outside Christian apologetics no trained historian accepts the conjecture that historians are warranted for accepting the so-called historicity of Jesus' resurrection. Most historians view a person returning from the dead on the third day as being a

3. Ferguson, "Scripture and Tradition," in Beeke et al., *Sola Scriptura*, 103.

4. Maddock, "Comparison of the Use," 116–18, 120.

supernatural explanation that is beyond the work of historians, and with good reason—they strive to preserve the highest standards in the academic study of history. There appears to be antithetical or inconsistent positions in contemporary apologetics regarding the historian's role. The beginning of the last chapter provided a good example: Apologists seem to believe that "spiritual truths" are beyond confirmation by historical standards, e.g., "when it comes to the spiritual truths in the New Testament, these cannot be confirmed using the tools available to historians, any more than those same tools can confirm the existence of black holes."[5] Reasonably, it can be deduced that spiritual truths and a person being raised from the dead (to fulfill prophecy) fit into the same category—the metaphysical or the supernatural. However, contemporaries argue that the supernatural can be confirmed by historians if that's where the evidence leads. A criterion for separating the two is not provided. There is no explanation for why spiritual truths are exempt from historical confirmations but prophecy-fulfilling resurrections are not. Still, scholars holding these controversial views would agree that the miraculous resurrection of Jesus Christ is not beyond the work of the theologian. Theologians can weigh the historical evidence regarding the resurrection and are only justified by faith in concluding it was God who raised Jesus from the dead, emphasizing Christianity as a historically based truthful religion. The phrase "historically based" is used because, for example, some aspects in the narratives contained within the Gospels—the existence of the historical Jesus and his crucifixion—can be and are evaluated by historians. The resurrection and Christ's atonement cannot be evaluated by historical methods. This epistemology must be evaluated by the theologian based on Scripture that supports the Christian faith.

5. Licona, "Licona's Statement," Summary, para. 2.

Bibliography

Aland, Barbara, et al., eds. *The Greek New Testament: A Reader's Edition* (UBS). Stuttgart: Deutsche Bibelgesellschaft, 2014.

Barnes, Timothy D. "Emperors and Bishops of Constantinople (324–431)." In *Christianity, Democracy, and the Shadow of Constantine*, edited by Demacopoulos George E. and Papanikolaou Aristotle, 175–201. New York: Fordham University Press, 2017. http://www.jstor.org/stable/j.ctt1gn6b41.12.

Becker, Carl. "Everyman His Own Historian." In *The Modern Historiography Reader: Western Sources*, edited by Adam Budd, 221–36. New York: Routledge, 2009. Originally published in *American Historical Review* 37 (January 1932).

Beeke, Joel R. et al. *Sola Scriptura: The Protestant Position on the Bible*. Stanford, FL: Reformation Trust, 2009.

Blue Letter Bible. "Philippians 2 (NIV)." https://www.blueletterbible.org/niv/phl/2/1/s_1105001.

Boyd, Gregory A. "Interpreting Scripture as God's Word: The Cruciform Hermeneutic and the Theological Interpretation of Scripture." In *The Crucifixion of the Warrior of God*, 1:513–52. Minneapolis: Augsburg Fortress, 2017. https://www.jstor.org/stable/j.ctt1kgqv00.16.

Brown, Raymond E. *An Introduction to the New Testament: The Abridged Edition*. Edited by Marion L. Soards. New Haven, CT: Yale University Press, 2016. http://www.jstor.org/stable/j.ctvggx32v.

Brundage, Anthony. *Going to the Sources*. Malden, MA: Wiley & Sons, 2013.

Bryce, Raymond. "Christ as Second Adam: Girardian Mimesis Redeemed." *New Blackfriars* 93/1045 (2012) 358–70. http://www.jstor.org/stable/43251628.

Charles P. Arand, James A. Nestingen, and Robert Kolb. "A History of the Ancient Creedal Texts: Apostles, Nicene, and Athanasian." In *The Lutheran Confessions: History and Theology of The Book of Concord*, 15–40. Minneapolis: Augsburg Fortress, 2012.

Cook, Albert E. "The Bible as God's Word." *The Biblical World* 42/3 (September 1913) 127–39. https://www.jstor.org/stable/3149148.

Cousland, J. R. C. "Authorship, Date, and Place of Composition." In *The New Oxford Annotated Bible: With Apocrypha*, edited by Michael D. Coogan et al., 1781. New York: Oxford University Press, 2018.

Bauer, W., F. W. Danker, W. F. Arndt, and F. W. Gingrich. *Greek-English Lexicon of the New Testament and Other Early Christian Literature* (BDAG). 3rd ed. Chicago: University of Chicago Press, 1999.

Benoit-Dominique, de La Soujeole. "The Church Is Apostolic." In *Introduction to the Mystery of the Church*, 590–624. Translated by Michael J. Miller. Washington, DC: Catholic University of America Press, 2014. http://www.jstor.org/stable/j.ctt9qdqm2.25.

Dunn, James D. G. *Jesus Remembered: Christianity in the Making*. Vol. 1. Grand Rapids: Eerdmans, 2003.

Ehrman, Bart D. *How Jesus Became God: The Exaltation of a Jewish Preacher from Galilee*. New York: HarperCollins, 2014.

———. "The New Testament Canon of Didymus the Blind." *Vigiliae Christianae* 37 (1983) 1–21.

Ehrman, Bart D., and Michael R. Licona. "Are the Gospels Historically Reliable? Part 1." February 21, 2018, Morgan Hall, Kennesaw, Georgia. https://www.youtube.com/watch?v=h7-QljtixEM.

Elwell, Walter A., ed. *Evangelical Dictionary of Theology*. 2nd ed. Grand Rapids: Baker Academic, 2001.

Erickson, Millard J. *Christian Theology*. 3rd ed. Grand Rapids: Baker Academic, 2013.

Ferguson, Everett. *Church History: From Christ to the Pre-Reformation*. Vol. 1. 2nd ed. Grand Rapids: Zondervan, 2013.

———. "Irenaeus' Proof of the Apostolic Preaching and Early Catechetical Instruction." In *The Early Church at Work and Worship*, vol. 2, *Catechesis, Baptism, Eschatology, and Martyrdom*, 1–17. Cambridge: James Clarke, 2014. http://www.jstor.org/stable/j.ctt1cgf67k.5.

Gilderhus, Mark T. *History and Historians: A Historiographical Introduction*. Upper Saddle River, NJ: Prentice Hall, 2010.

Hart, D. G. "Fundamentalism, Inerrancy, and the Biblical Scholarship of J. Gresham Machen." *Journal of Presbyterian History* 75/1 (Spring 1997) 13–28. https://www.jstor.org/stable/23335439.

Haskell, Yasmin. "The 'Tristia' of a Greek Refugee: Michael Marullus and the Politics of Latin Subjectivity After the Fall of Constantinople (1453)." *Proceedings of the Cambridge Philological Society* 44 (1998) 110–36. http://www.jstor.org/stable/44696768.

Hellerman, Joseph H. *Philippians: The Exegetical Guide to the Greek New Testament*. Nashville: B&H Academic, 2015.

Herrin, Judith. "The City of Constantine." In *Byzantium: The Surprising Life of a Medieval Empire*, 3–11. Princeton, NJ: Princeton University Press, 2007. http://www.jstor.org/stable/j.ctv6zdbvf.6.

Holmes, Michael W., trans. *The Apostolic Fathers: Greek Texts and English Translations*. 3rd ed. Grand Rapids: Baker Academic, 2007.

Hopkins, Keith. "Taxes and Trade in the Roman Empire (200 B.C.–A.D. 400)." *Journal of Roman Studies* 70 (1980) 101–25. doi:10.2307/299558.

Irenaeus. *Against the Heresies. Book 1.* Translated by Dominic J. Unger. Ancient Christian Writers 64. Mahwah, NJ: Newman, 1992.

Licona, Michael R. "Licona's Statement: The New Testament Gospels Are Historically Reliable Accounts of Jesus." *The Best Schools*, 2016. https://thebestschools.org/special/ehrman-licona-dialogue-reliability-new-testament/licona-major-statement/.

———. *The Resurrection of Jesus: A New Historiographical Approach.* Downers Grove, IL: InterVarsity, 2010.

Livingstone, David N., and Mark A. Noll. "A Biblical Inerrantist as Evolutionist." *Journal* of *Presbyterian History* 80/3 (Fall 2002) 153–71. https://www.jstor.org/stable/23336691.

Maddock, Ian J. "A Comparison of the Use, Interpretation, and Application of the Inspired Word in the Printed Words of George Whitefield and John Wesley." In *Men of One Book: A Comparison of Two Methodist Preachers, John Wesley and George Whitefield*, 102–75. Cambridge: Lutterworth, 2011. https://www.jstor.org/stable/j.ctt1cgdvt3.8.

Mayne, Richard. "East and West in 1054." *Cambridge Historical Journal* 11/2 (1954) 133–48. http://www.jstor.org/stable/3021073.

McDonnell, Kilian. "Canon and Koinonia/communio: The Formation of the Canon as an Ecclesiological Process." *Gregorianum* 79/1 (1998) 29–54. http://www.jstor.org/stable/23580300.

McGrath, Alister E. *Historical Theology: An Introduction to the History of Christian Thought.* 2nd ed. Oxford: Wiley & Sons, 2013.

Metzger, Bruce M. *The Canon of the New Testament: Its Origins, Development, and Significance.* New York: Oxford University Press, 1987.

———. *The New Testament: Its Background, Growth, and Content.* 3rd ed. Nashville: Abingdon Press, 2003.

Meyer, Marvin W., ed. *The Nag Hammadi Scriptures: The Revised and Updated Translation of Sacred Gnostic Texts Complete in One Volume.* Intern. ed. New York: HarperCollins, 2009.

Moriarty, W. "1 Clement's View of Ministerial Appointments in the Early Church." *Vigiliae Christianae* 66/2 (2012) 115–38. http://www.jstor.org/stable/41480524.

Noble, Peter. "Hermann Sasse's Theology of Scripture and its Legacy in the LCA." *Lutheran Theological Journal* 51/3 (2017) 184–203.

Nolin, L. A. "The Briggs Controversy from a Catholic Standpoint." *North American Review* 157/442 (September 1893) 380–83. https://www.jstor.org/stable/25103205.

Olson, Roger E. *The Story of Christian Theology: Twenty Centuries of Tradition & Reform.* Downers Grove, IL: InterVarsity, 1999.

Osiek, Carolyn. "The Letter of Paul to the Philippians." In *The New Oxford Annotated Bible: With Apocrypha*, edited by Michael D. Coogan et al., 2099–100. New York: Oxford University Press, 2018.

Salzman, Michele Renee. "Leo's Liturgical Topography: Contestations for Space in Fifth-Century Rome." *Journal of Roman Studies* 103 (2013) 208–32. http://www.jstor.org/stable/43286785.

Satta, Ronald F. "The Case of Professor Charles A. Briggs: Inerrancy Affirmed." *Trinity Journal* 26/1 (Spring 2005) 69–90.

Schreiner, Thomas R. *Interpreting the Pauline Epistles*. 2nd ed. Grand Rapids: Baker Academic, 2011.

Shelly, Bruce L. *Church History in Plain Language*. 4th ed. Nashville: Thomas Nelson, 2013.

Steenberg, Irenaeus M. C. "Tracing the Irenaean Legacy." In *Irenaeus: Life, Scripture, Legacy*, edited by Sara Parvis and Paul Foster, 99–211. Minneapolis: Augsburg Fortress, 2012. http://www.jstor.org/stable/j.ctt22nm648.

Vine, W. E., Merrill F. Unger, and William White Jr. *Vine's Complete Expository Dictionary of Old and New Testament Words*. Nashville: Thomas Nelson, 1996.

Wallace, Daniel B. *Greek Grammar: Beyond the Basics: An Exegetical Syntax of the New Testament*. Grand Rapids: Zondervan, 1996.

Wiesner-Hanks, Merry E. *Early Modern Europe 1450–789*. 2nd ed. Cambridge: Cambridge University Press, 2013.

Worthing, Mark. "The Inerrancy of Scripture Debate within the LCA, 1966–1984: The Historical Background." *Lutheran Theological Journal* 51/2 (December 2017) 155–69.

www.ingramcontent.com/pod-product-compliance
Lightning Source LLC
LaVergne TN
LVHW020655100826
845148LV00012B/2498
9781666700930